BREAKING
into BANKING

CRACKING THE CODE ON LAUNCHING

a successful career

IN **COMMERCIAL BANKING**

ANDY KEUSAL

CreateSpace Independent Publishing Platform, North Charleston, SC

Printed in the United States of America

LCCN: 2015901648

ISBN: 150777771X
ISBN-13: 978-150777-771-8

Praise for *Breaking into Banking*:

"Andy helped me navigate the complex world of credit and commercial banking when I was hired by a large regional bank after college. His training and support helped me to obtain a solid foundation for a successful career in banking on both the credit and lending sides of the organization. *Breaking into Banking* will provide you with the introduction you need to help you start your own successful career in commercial banking at any level."

- Nicole V. Callam, Sr. VP Commercial Banking, FirstMerit Bank

"Andy hired me and helped me break into banking immediately after I graduated from a liberal arts college. His solid training helped me to master the basics of commercial banking, and now I'm enjoying a career at a Private Equity firm in New York City. I highly recommend *Breaking into Banking* for anyone just starting their career."

- Tony Hokayem, Sr. VP, Colbeck Capital

"I was hired by Andy right out of college. His vast experience and ability to relate and educate propelled me into a very successful 10-year banking career in Chicago. Although I was a Finance and Accounting major I wish I would've had this 'pre-training' opportunity, especially with someone like Andy. I highly recommend him and his training to anyone interested in banking."

Alex Reo, Financial Representative, Northwestern Mutual

ANDY KEUSAL

*This book is dedicated
to my wife, Kirsten:
Thank you for your steadfast
love and encouragement
during this project, as always.*

TABLE OF CONTENTS

ANDY KEUSAL

INTRODUCTION

What This Book Will Do For You

If you are considering starting a career in commercial banking, this book is for you. I wish I would have had a book like this when I started my banking career. I had been hired as a Credit Analyst and was glad to have a job in a new industry. However, in my first week on the job, I quickly realized that I was not adequately prepared to begin doing the work expected of me. While that is true of almost anyone in a new job, commercial credit work can be especially intimidating because of its complexity and the risk-oriented nature of the work. The bank that hired me was counting on me to provide accurate information and insightful analysis to help it make good credit decisions. There was so much for me to learn, and so little time.

I wrote this book because I want to help you to start better than I did. It is not intended to be a credit training manual – there are plenty of those around, and most of them are pretty boring. Instead, think of me as your personal mentor and consider this book to be an exclusive conversation between the two of us. But why should you listen to me?

Because I've been there, and I know what your bank really wants from you. In my 18-year commercial banking career, I have interviewed, hired, trained, and managed hundreds of new Credit

Analysts. Many of them have gone on to have lucrative banking careers all across the country. I also helped to build one of the nation's premier credit training programs at a large Midwest regional bank. So I understand what you really need to know to be successful, and I want to give it to you in this book. You can avoid the struggles I experienced, and you can hit the ground running, making a smooth transition into your new job.

This book is for you if:

- You are graduating from college and want to get a job in commercial banking
- You already work for a bank in some other capacity and want to transition into commercial banking
- You are dissatisfied with your current job in another field and think banking might be a better fit

The information in this book will give you a decided edge on the competition, helping you to get a better understanding of the industry and what you need to do to be successful in it. Because I want you to grasp the *reality* of the banking world over textbook portrayals of the business, I will:

- Give you some background about the banking business
- Explain the *business* of banking – how banks actually make money
- Introduce you to the role of the commercial banker
- Summarize the basics of commercial credit: underwriting,

loan structuring, the loan approval process, and portfolio monitoring

- Provide information about other departments in commercial banking and explain how you can effectively interact with them
- Help you know if you are a good fit in this industry
- **Let you test-drive your new job by showing you a typical day in your life as a Credit Analyst (page 130)**
- Explore the career paths open to you once you master your initial Credit Analyst role

In each chapter, I will introduce you to key concepts and related banking terminology, without getting too deep into the weeds. There is plenty more to be said about each topic, but for now I simply want you to know enough to absorb more thorough training when it comes your way. This book is about recognizing the big pieces of the puzzle and how they fit together.

As an extra bonus, I've also included a few tips on interviewing that will help you get your foot in the door and differentiate yourself from other candidates, so you can get the banking job you really want.

After reading this book, you will know that commercial banking is the right career for you, and you will have a running start toward launching your career and achieving great success in it.

Let's get started!

Chapter 1

THE BUSINESS OF BANKING

Congratulations! Just by picking up this book, you have set yourself apart as someone who truly wants to succeed. You have an interest in commercial banking, so reading this book will help you to better understand the industry and your place in it. Experienced baby boomer bankers are beginning to retire in record numbers, so there is tremendous opportunity for energetic people to step in and fill that void. The banking industry requires creative solutions to its unique challenges, and the information in the pages that follow will help you be part of the solution to those challenges.

Before jumping into details about the day-to-day life of a banker, you probably want to know a bit about the industry itself. How long have banks been around, and why do we need them? More importantly, would *your* experience, education, and skills allow you to enjoy a prosperous banking career?

With those questions in mind, I have dedicated this first chapter to introducing you to the commercial banking industry. You want to have a clear picture of what banks do, how they make money, and how they serve their customers. If you have a Finance degree or retail banking experience some of the material in this chapter will already be familiar to you. After quickly laying this important foundation here, I will jump into meatier content in subsequent chapters that will specifically help you in your Credit Analyst role.

People have always sought a safe haven for their money, so centuries ago bankers figured out a profit could be made by offering a secure repository for that money while lending it out to others who were in need of capital. When done responsibly, banking has always been an honorable profession. And especially after the financial meltdown of 2008, our economy desperately needs good banks and smart bankers.

Relationships and Risk

Before we begin talking about the components of your job, understanding a bit about how banks actually make money is important – that is, the business of banking. At its core, banking is about two things: *building relationships* and *managing risk*.

These relationships are both internal (between you and your co-workers) and external (between you and the bank's customers, vendors, regulators, and others). You will be off to a solid start if you sincerely care about getting this right. While much of this book is about finance, accounting, lending, and critical analysis, being a successful banker is fundamentally about successfully connecting with the right people. Since making these connections is so important to achieving your long-term career goals, I will help you understand who these people are and how to do this.

Banking is also about managing risk. While this is true of almost all businesses to some degree, it's especially true of banks because they handle other people's *money*. If we define risk as the possibility of something bad or dangerous happening, then here is a quick overview of some types of risk banks must manage:

- *Credit* – The risk that borrowers won't repay their loans as agreed. This is the big one that has caused many banks to fail, so it is the primary focus of this book

- *Operational* – The risk that a bank's systems or processes would fail, thus impacting both customers and employees as the bank would not be able to deliver its products or services

- *Reputational* – The risk of damage done by adverse public opinion

- *Legal* – The risk of incurring penalties and fines arising from litigation

- *Market* – The risk of interest rate fluctuations impacting the bank's profitability

- *Regulatory* – The risk of being fined, penalized, or shut down by not adhering to rules and laws the various governing bodies that oversee banks have established

I will touch on each of these types of risk later, but for now I want you to realize that much of banking is about identifying when these risks are present (covered in Chapter 3) and knowing how to mitigate them (Chapter 4).

How Banks Make Money

Understanding that relationships and risk management are critical to the business of banking, let's now turn our attention to how the business actually works. Every company must provide a product or service that customers need, and then it must find a way to earn a profit doing this. If you were going to work at a bakery, the business would make money by purchasing raw materials, following a recipe to make delicious food, and then selling the finished product to hungry customers. If a roofing contractor hired you, the business model would be much different. You would be providing a service, and if you did it well – showing up at the customer's home on time and fixing the leaky roof – then you would be helping your employer earn a profit based on the service you provided.

But what about a bank? Banks are businesses, and they too must profitably sell products or services to stay in business. You might never have thought about it because your only experience with your bank might have been opening a checking or savings account. That didn't seem much like a "sale," at least not like either of the two previous examples. But banks do make money from servicing their customers, and the better you understand how this happens, the more effective you will be in your job.

Let me begin by making a basic distinction between the two sides of a bank: *retail* and *commercial*. The retail side of a bank focuses on servicing individual consumers – people and families – and it delivers this service through a network of branches and Automated Teller Machines (ATMs). Almost everyone needs a checking account and a debit or credit card for managing personal cash flow and paying bills. Occasionally, personal loans are needed to buy more expensive items like a car or a home. All of these products are offered through the retail part of a bank.

The focus of this book is commercial banking, which deals not with individuals but with companies. Like consumers, businesses need a place to keep their cash on deposit, and they frequently need to borrow money, but their needs are usually much larger and more complex than those of consumers. Because commercial banking is so different from retail banking, the skills needed to be successful on this side of the bank are also very different. You'll see the contrast between retail and commercial banking through more examples in later chapters.

Since you are reading this book, you obviously are more interested in learning about the commercial side of banking, so let's look at how banks make money here. Simply put, banks make money primarily two ways:

- Interest rate spread – Buying low and selling high

• Fee income – Including origination fees, annual fees, waiver fees, and product fees

First, let's look at interest rate spread. At the end of the chapter, we'll discuss how banks make money from fees and why this is especially important in a low interest rate environment.

Interest Rate Spread

If you have ever watched the classic Christmas movie "It's a Wonderful Life," then you have already been exposed to the business of banking. I'm sure you will be a notch or two sharper than fumbling Uncle Billy (who probably could have used this book). Remember the scene where there is a "run on the bank," and the customers of the Savings and Loan storm into the banking office, demanding to withdraw all of their money? They had deposited it, and now they wanted it back. George Bailey tried to explain to them that their money wasn't in some vault in the back room where they could simply walk in and retrieve it. Rather, their deposited funds had been loaned out to their neighbors who used that money to build their homes.

I don't know what interest rates were back in those days, but I'm confident that the interest rate the Savings and Loan charged its customers on their home loans was higher than the rate the customers were receiving on their deposits. In today's terms, you may be earning 1% interest on the money you have in a savings account at your bank, but if you want to borrow money from that same bank to buy a home, you might have to pay 4% interest on that loan. Why? The bank needs to earn a profit to stay in business. The difference in those two interest rates – what the bank pays on deposits and what it collects on loans – is how it makes money.

Buy Low…

The first way banks strive to improve this "interest rate spread" is by paying as little interest as possible on customers' deposits. If you have a checking account, you have probably noticed on your monthly bank statement that you are credited with a whopping $0.01 interest on the last day of each month. If you live to be as old as Methuselah, this might compound and amount to a substantial sum one day, but don't try holding your breath that long. Less than a generation ago, savings accounts paid 8-10% interest, but in today's low rate environment, you won't earn much more on your savings accounts than on your checking account.

This is bad news for both consumers and for businesses that have excess cash, but good news for banks since it lowers their "cost of funds" – what it costs them to obtain the money that they lend. Every business wants to buy or make its product as inexpensively as possible to improve its profit margin, and banking is no different. What makes banking unique is that the product banks sell is *money*, and the primary supplier of that product is not an overseas manufacturing company. Strange as it sounds, a bank's primary product suppliers are *its own customers*! Banks essentially have to buy their product – money – from their customers, and they do this by paying them interest on their deposits. What is even more unusual is that as soon as banks sell their product to a customer (lend them money), they immediately ask them to start giving it back to them. Go figure.

... And Sell High

The other way for banks to improve their spreads is to charge as high an interest rate as possible when lending money. The free market (competition among banks) limits how high these rates can go, but be assured bankers will always try to negotiate the highest rate possible while still remaining competitive. Commercial bankers refer to interest rate spread in terms of "basis points" where a basis point is equal to one hundredth (1/100) of a percent. For example, in the previous scenario, if a bank's average cost of funds (the interest rate it paid its depositors) is 1% and it charges a customer 4% interest on a loan, then its spread is 3% or 300 basis points, expressed as "300 bps," on that loan. A simplified example of this is illustrated in Figure 1.1.

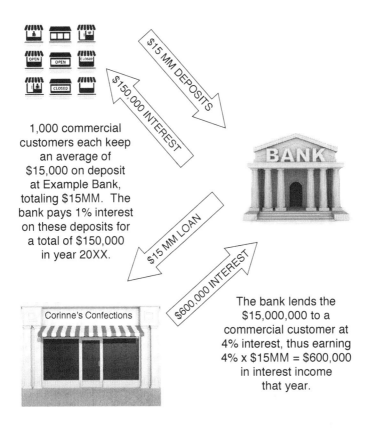

1,000 commercial customers each keep an average of $15,000 on deposit at Example Bank, totaling $15MM. The bank pays 1% interest on these deposits for a total of $150,000 in year 20XX.

The bank lends the $15,000,000 to a commercial customer at 4% interest, thus earning 4% x $15MM = $600,000 in interest income that year.

Net interest income earned by the bank in year 20XX
from these customers is $600,000 - $150,000 = $450,000

Figure 1.1

Here I want to mention briefly that the relationship between deposits and loans is not as simple in reality as I have just explained. A practice called "fractional-reserve banking" allows banks to lend out far more money than they actually have in customer deposits. A healthy debate exists as to whether this is a sound practice, but that debate, and a detailed explanation of how fractional-reserve banking works, is beyond the scope of this book.

With this understanding of how banks earn interest rate spread, you can see why the motto of commercial bankers is, "Every basis point counts." While this is true of a $15,000 car loan or a $150,000 loan for a motor home, imagine the impact of each basis point on a commercial loan of $15,000,000 for a business to purchase a fleet of delivery trucks. Although banks make more consumer vehicle loans each year than they make commercial loans, the large dollar amount of the average commercial loan makes interest rate spread that much more critical.

Fee Income

As I mentioned earlier and as you can see in Figure 1.2, banks earn revenue from two primary sources: interest rate spread and fee income. I have already explained how interest rate spread works, so now let's look at how banks earn money from fees.

Since you probably have a checking account and you may have purchased a home, you are already familiar with some of the fees banks charge their customers on the retail side of the business. Examples include:

• Monthly fees for having paper account statements mailed to you

- Overdraft fees if you don't keep enough money in your account to cover checks you have written

- Application fees or underwriting fees when you apply for a home mortgage loan

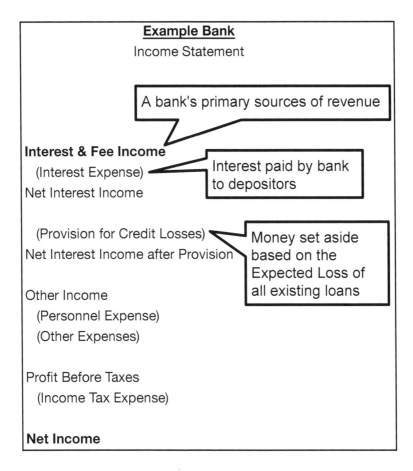

Figure 1.2

Because commercial banking deals with larger account balances and bigger loan amounts than in retail banking, opportunities for earning fees can be substantial, so familiarizing yourself with some of these types of fees is important. I will also explain to you how banks view this fee income very differently from interest income and why understanding the difference is critical.

Origination Fees

To understand the most common type of commercial banking fee, let's go back to our example of the business looking to borrow $15,000,000 to purchase a fleet of new delivery trucks. In the next chapter, I will discuss in detail the reasons why businesses borrow money. For now, let's assume that this company is expanding into a new geographic region, so they need more vehicles to get their products to their customers in that area of the country. If the bank agrees to lend the money to the business, the loan agreement will typically include a one-time fee to be paid to the bank up front – that is, at the time the loan is closed. This is called a "commitment" (origination) fee and is usually no more than 1% (100 bps) of the total loan amount. For example, the business borrowing $15,000,000 to buy the new trucks might pay an origination fee of 50 bps, which would be equal to $15,000,000 X 0.005 = $75,000.

This fee income increases the profitability of the transaction for the bank. But even more importantly, the bank earns all of the fee income *immediately* with no risk of the customer defaulting as with repaying the loan. Nor does the bank have to concern itself with market risk – movement in interest rates over time, the yield curve, or any other unknown future factor. The fee income is pure profit, incrementally improving the bank's bottom line (net income) without taking any additional credit risk.

Even though commercial banking involves a "business-to-business" relationship between a company and its bank, understand that it is still a relationship between *people*. Businesses are owned and run by human beings, and so are banks. As with any successful long-term relationship, a commercial banking relationship must be beneficial for both parties involved and will undoubtedly involve some negotiating on both sides, especially when the business has a new borrowing request. In these negotiations, commercial bankers will often ask about the "quid pro quo" – a Latin phrase meaning, "Something for something." That is, if a bank is going to take on additional risk by lending more money to the business, then the business will have to compensate the bank in some way.

For example, if the borrower shown in Figure 1.1 is pushing for a lower interest rate (and they usually do), then the bank could compromise by lowering the rate by 10 bps (from 4.00% to 3.90%) but including a 20 bps origination fee. The company saves $15,000 per year in interest expense in exchange for coming up with $30,000 in cash at closing. In the long run, the bank makes less money this way, but "a bird in the hand is worth two in the bush" – the bank gets a bigger chunk of cash immediately in lieu of potentially larger interest income in the future. This is very similar to the concept of a consumer paying "points" to buy down the interest rate on a home mortgage loan.

Annual Fees

Many businesses like to have lines of credit available to them as part of their commercial banking relationship. I'll explain more about how these work in Chapters 2 and 4, but for now think of a line of credit as a credit card with a very high limit. Banks typically make these available to customers for a period of one year with the intention of renewing them annually as long as the borrower remains creditworthy. Many borrowers are willing to pay an annual fee to keep these lines of credit available to them, which provides a second source of fee income for the bank.

That's Going to Cost You – Waiver Fees

Now that I have introduced you to origination fees and annual fees, I'll illustrate a third type of fee income by giving you a peek into a typical day in my home. My wife and I have eight children under twelve years old. As you might imagine, there is always plenty of work to do, so once the children are old enough, they are assigned daily chores. For the older ones, we typically write down what they are expected to do as well as the consequences of not doing so. For example, they must sweep the kitchen floor after dinner, and if they don't do it without being reminded, then they have to pay us 25 cents from their piggy bank (and of course they still have to sweep the floor). This arrangement motivates them to keep their end of the agreement.

Similarly, banks charge fees when customers don't live up to their loan agreements. I will explain loan covenants in greater depth in Chapter 4, but for now just think of a covenant as a written agreement specifying something that the customer must do (or not do) over the course of repaying the loan. If the borrower doesn't keep its end of the deal, the bank may choose to "call the loan" – require payment in full. More likely, it will elect to waive the covenant default but charge the customer a one-time "waiver fee." Again, this cash is collected in full immediately and thus carries no additional credit risk.

Product Fees

One final example of non-interest income banks earn comes from Treasury Management services. This simply refers to the numerous products banks offer to help business customers manage their cash (discussed in more detail in Chapter 7). Just as consumers pay a few dollars per month to maintain a checking account and a debit card, businesses also pay monthly fees for these types of services. The products are more complex than what retail consumers need, so they are appropriately more expensive. They help companies to keep their businesses running smoothly, and they provide additional profitability for the bank. Some businesses never need to borrow money, but they use their banks solely for these cash management services. These relationships are very valuable to the bank because of their profitability with no credit risk.

When is an Asset not an Asset?

As I wrap up this discussion of the business of banking, I want to point out that a bank's financial statements are very different than those of most businesses. As a Credit Analyst, you will spend plenty of time analyzing the balance sheets and income statements of companies in various industries. Their balance sheets will show the cash they have on deposit at their bank as an *asset*, and the outstanding balance on their bank loan as a *liability*. Conversely, a bank's balance sheet will reflect deposits as a liability. The bank owes that money to its customers and will have to pay it back whenever the customers come into the branch to withdraw their money (unless Uncle Billy is running the teller window that day).

Accordingly, when a bank loans money to a company, it considers that loan to be an *asset*, not a liability. Why? Because the bank is in the business of lending money, and its loans produce cash flow for the bank by generating interest income until they are paid off by the borrowers. Like any successful business, a bank wants to put its assets to work generating revenue for the company, and a bank's most productive assets are its loans to its customers. If this concept is new to you or seems counterintuitive, you are not alone. It will make more sense as we move through the book, and I will explain it more fully in Chapter 6.

Summary

In conclusion, remember that banks are businesses too, so their profitability is based largely on how much fee income they generate and how much interest income they earn. But the biggest threat to a bank's profitability is neither declining fee income nor narrow interest rate spreads. It is the risk of making bad loans – lending money to businesses and then not being repaid as agreed. This topic – credit risk – is so critical for you to grasp that I'll devote an entire chapter (3) to it when I discuss underwriting. But first let's look at the reasons why businesses borrow money in the first place.

Key Takeaways

Successful Bankers:

- **Build Relationships**
- **Manage Risk**

Banks Make Money Two Ways:

- **Interest Rate Spread on Loans**
- **Fees from Products and Services**

ANDY KEUSAL

Chapter 2

WHY DO BUSINESSES BORROW MONEY?

When I was a new Credit Analyst beginning my banking career, I would not have understood why this chapter would even be necessary. Wasn't it obvious why companies borrow money? Because they need more of it! I soon learned that this answer wouldn't suffice when my credit officer asked me for a more detailed explanation. Borrowing causes vary, and each requires a specific type of loan. Most of your time, especially as a new Credit Analyst, will be spent dealing with customers that want to borrow money from your bank. Given its obvious importance, let's dig a little deeper into the topic of borrowing causes.

Capital Expenditures

Let's assume that you have recently purchased your first automobile. Even if you are a hard worker and have been earning money for a while, you probably didn't have enough money saved to pay cash for that vehicle. Smaller expenditures like groceries and clothing could be funded out of your regular monthly cash flow, but the vehicle purchase may have required a car loan simply because of the size of the expense and the longer "useful life" of the asset you were buying. And even if you did have just enough cash on hand to make the big purchase, you might not have wanted to drain all of your liquidity, leaving yourself with no cash available for other expenses. Longer-term assets like cars and homes are best financed with long-term debt that will be paid off over a number of years.

Businesses often borrow money for the exact same reason. They want or need to purchase something expensive, and they don't want to burn a big chunk of their available cash to buy it. The most common example of this is a manufacturing company that purchases new equipment to increase its production capacity or to replace older equipment that is obsolete or no longer working. Equipment is expensive and has a useful life of many years, so businesses like to borrow money from their bank to finance these purchases, which are typically referred to as capital expenditures (CapEx). Other examples of capital expenditures include purchases of fixed assets like vehicles, forklifts, computers, furniture, and fixtures. For larger businesses, these might even include corporate aircraft, ships, or earth-moving equipment like bulldozers and backhoes.

Since you were smart enough to buy my book, I'm guessing

that if you did finance your car, you didn't charge it on your credit card. Aside from the higher interest rate you would have paid, you knew that credit cards are best used for short-term borrowing needs, which you intend to pay back quickly. Conversely, a car that you intend to drive for five years might best be financed with a 5-year loan, matching the life of the asset with the life (tenor) of the loan.

Similarly, capital expenditures are best financed by "term loans," which are structured very much the same as the car loan in the previous example. All of the funds needed for the purchase are disbursed to the borrower at the time of the purchase and are expected to be paid back in monthly installments over a period of a few years, depending on the useful life of the asset. For example, computers might be financed for only three years given how quickly they become obsolete. The loan for the corporate airplane, however, might be paid off over a ten-year period since it will still be in the air long after the computers have been replaced by newer technology.

Real Estate

Businesses also frequently borrow to purchase real estate. Younger companies typically rent office or retail space in the early years of their operation, but as they grow and become more profitable, they often look to purchase a building in which to run their business. Again, given the large price tag of commercial real estate and the expected life of these buildings, companies usually borrow money to finance these assets. The paperwork is a bit more complex when purchasing real estate than when buying a car, but the basic structure of the commercial mortgage loan looks very similar to term debt. The full amount of the loan is disbursed from the bank to the borrower at the time of the purchase, and then the borrower begins making monthly payments.

The biggest difference between a loan for real estate and one for capital expenditures is that the repayment (amortization) of the real estate loan will be over a longer period of time (20-25 years) since buildings are expected to be useful assets longer than computers, cars, or even airplanes. I'll expand on this concept in the chapter on Loan Structuring.

Lines of Credit

Now imagine that after purchasing that new car, you are hired into the commercial banking training program at the best bank in your town. The salary is even better than you expected; best of all, the offer includes a good signing bonus. This bonus will allow you to buy some furniture and start building your professional wardrobe. You can finally quit waiting tables, and you'll have your evenings free. The only problem is that the bank doesn't want you to start working until next month, so you won't get your signing bonus or your first paycheck for about six weeks. How will you pay for those four new business suits you will need for the first week on the job?

Maybe you have been disciplined enough to save those tips, and you have enough cash on hand to make the purchase out of pocket. Or perhaps your parents or friends can help. If not, then clearly this is a short-term financing need, so this might be a good time to pull out your credit card. Your cash need is only for a few weeks, and you have a clearly defined timeline and source of repayment. If you are going to borrow, then using your credit card makes a lot more sense than going to the bank and applying for a 5-year loan. Besides, you don't know exactly how much money you will need until you are at the clothing store, so your credit card gives you the flexibility to borrow only what you need and no more, assuming that you don't spend more than your $2,000 limit.

The other attractive feature of your credit card is that you can borrow using the card (draw it up) and then pay it down whenever you want to, assuming you make at least the minimum monthly payment. In our example, you would pay off the entire balance when you receive your signing bonus. Your credit card would have then served its short-term purpose well, and it would be available again up to your approved limit whenever another short-term borrowing need arose.

The commercial banking equivalent of the personal credit card is a "working capital line of credit." Since this chapter is about why businesses borrow money, I will explain why a company would use a line of credit to borrow from its bank.

Seasonality

Consider Hannah's Hi-Quality Horsey Hats, a distributor of fine equestrian headwear. Hannah sells her products year-round, but 80% of her sales are made in October each year when the annual

Quarter Horse Congress comes to her hometown. To capitalize on this, Hannah must buy plenty of inventory in July and August to stock the shelves in her store, knowing that she will have most of it sold by the end of October. She has product expertise, she knows the needs of her customers, and she is a terrific salesperson. Her only problem? She doesn't have enough cash to buy the inventory.

This is a perfect opportunity for Hannah to use her company's working capital line of credit. She can borrow money as she needs it throughout the summer months to make purchases from her suppliers, pay interest on her outstanding balance for only a few months, and then pay off the balance once the Congress is over. If Hannah needs to borrow again in November to stock up on Christmas items, she can use the line of credit again, knowing that she will pay it off in January. This type of seasonality is a great example of why businesses borrow money using lines of credit.

Financing Accounts Receivable and Inventory

Most of Hannah's customers are individuals and families who spend less than $100 per purchase, and they typically pay with cash or credit cards, so Hannah gets her cash almost immediately. But what if Hannah also had large equestrian centers across her state that ordered larger quantities of her headwear every month? These business-to-business sales usually are not paid in cash, but rather the customer asks Hannah to invoice them, and they promise to pay her within 30 days. These IOUs, or "Accounts Receivable," are from good companies that Hannah has dealt with for years. She trusts that they will pay her what they owe her, but a few customers always delay mailing their checks until the date they are due. And while Hannah is waiting for that money, she has to pay her suppliers, who aren't as patient as she is.

This illustrates another very common need for a business to use its line of credit: to "finance Accounts Receivable." That is, the business borrows money from its bank to pay its suppliers ("Accounts Payable") and pays the line of credit down as soon as its Accounts Receivable are collected. The three accounts I've described in these examples – Inventory, Accounts Receivable, and Accounts Payable – are often called the "working capital accounts" on a company's balance sheet. That is why the type of loan businesses use to finance them is called a working capital line of credit.

So businesses borrow money long-term for capital expenditures and real estate, and they borrow short-term to finance working capital assets. Using term loans, mortgage loans, and lines of credit, respectively, to meet these borrowing needs, banks play a vital role in helping companies to be successful. You can see from these simple examples that many businesses would not survive for long without access to these basic, but critical banking products.

The borrowing needs I've explained in the first part of this chapter are certainly the most common ones you will see as a commercial banker, but they are not the only ones. Companies will borrow money to fund the start-up of their operations, to acquire another business, to buy out an owner, or to fill a short-term financing gap. The rest of this chapter is devoted to explaining each of these borrowing needs and suggesting the most appropriate type of loan to meet each need.

Start-ups

You have probably heard the saying, "It takes money to make money." While there are exceptions to this rule, every successful business was once a brand new enterprise. Most of these start-up ventures needed a lot of capital to get off the ground. Why? New businesses need capital for many reasons, but I'll highlight the three most common: working capital, fixed assets, and operating expenses.

Earlier in this chapter, I explained how many companies use working capital lines of credit to buy inventory and to finance

Accounts Receivable – that is, to pay their bills while they wait to collect on IOUs from their customers. These financing needs are particularly acute in the case of a new business. A brand new company doesn't have the benefit of having generated cash flow and profit for the past few years, so if it wants

to stock its shelves with inventory, it often has to borrow money to do so.

And since the new company has no track record or payment history with its suppliers, they may not be inclined to wait as long to be paid since they view the new business as a greater credit risk. That is, because the suppliers know that a high percentage of start-ups fail and they don't want to be left holding the proverbial bag, they may demand payment sooner than they would from companies with solid payment histories. The new business would typically use its working capital line of credit in this situation to finance its initial inventory purchases and to be sure it can pay its suppliers promptly if collection of accounts receivable is slow.

Remember that not all businesses buy or manufacture inventory. Service providers such as law firms, consultants, and window cleaners don't need to stock their shelves like retailers do, and they don't need to buy raw materials like a manufacturer would. Companies like these generally have less of a need for working capital financing and may never even need a line of credit.

Business Acquisitions

In contrast to start-up businesses, mature companies with high market penetration often try to grow by acquiring other companies. In some instances, they are looking to buy a competitor, thus acquiring that competitor's customers as well as its assets. In other cases, the acquiring company wants to expand into adjacent geographic markets or to buy a business that offers a product or service complimentary to its own. Whatever the motive for the acquisition, these transactions are usually expensive and are typically financed by bank debt.

Similar to capital expenditures, acquisitions involve the purchase of long-term assets (other businesses), and thus they require long-term financing – usually a term loan. Again, all required funds for the acquisition would be disbursed up front at the time of the purchase, and repayment would consist of monthly or quarterly payments over a number of years.

Note that the expected source of repayment would be completely different in this case than when a company borrows under its working capital line of credit. In acquisition financing, the acquiring company expects the addition of new customers or new markets to increase its profitability, thus generating extra cash flow over many years to service the debt. Conversely, when Hannah borrows on her line of credit to purchase equestrian headwear in August, she expects to sell those products within 90 days and to repay the borrowings immediately with the cash generated from those sales.

Owner Buyouts

Another common reason why businesses borrow money from banks is to buy out the ownership interest of one of the principals of the business. Consider the case of Matthews Mansions, a company that builds and remodels residential homes. Mr. Daniel Matthews started the business over thirty years ago when his two sons, Luke and Mark, were small. Over time, Mr. Matthews involved his sons in various aspects of the company's operations, and now each of them is grown and owns a small part of the company. Dad has now decided to retire from the daily operations of the company, and since his sons would like to maintain family ownership of the business, they need to pay Dad for his share of the company.

Again, the company is not likely to have enough cash on hand to finance the proposed buyout, so the business would approach its bank with a borrowing request for the transaction. Bankers refer to this as restructuring the balance sheet (recapitalization). After the transaction, the company's balance sheet is weaker (more debt and less equity), but Dad now has additional cash in his pocket, and his sons each own a greater share of the business. These types of transactions are common, so you will want to understand how they work and why companies borrow money to get them done.

Bridge Loans

A few years ago, my family and I moved from a home on a small lot in the suburbs to a home on a 5-acre property in the country. The best part was that our property was bisected by a beautiful creek that meandered behind our home, separating the front half from what we started calling the "back property." When we began clearing the back property of trees and brush, I decided it would be an ideal site for a small orchard. The only problem was that there was no way to get from the front half to the back property unless we wanted to wade through the creek, which wasn't a good long-term solution given that I needed to get a mower back there.

The obvious solution? Hire a contractor to build a sturdy bridge over the creek – and that's exactly what I did. And how did I finance it? No, it wasn't a bridge loan. (Sorry – that was a trick question.) In fact, bridge loans have absolutely nothing to do with building bridges but have everything to do with helping companies get from one financial situation to another, usually in a short period of time. Bridge loans are also called "gap loans" or "swing loans" and are typically made when a more permanent financing source or some specific event is expected to pay it off within a year.

For example, consider a company that has outgrown its current manufacturing facility, so it is seeking to sell it and buy a larger building to accommodate its growth. The company finds an ideal new facility at a fair price and wants to take advantage of the opportunity to purchase it. But the situation is complicated when the prospective buyer of the company's original property can't close on the deal for nine months, thus tying up our company's equity for a short time. This is an ideal situation for the business to approach its bank for a bridge loan.

Unlike the other borrowing needs I've discussed, this borrower cannot repay the loan by selling inventory, collecting receivables, or earning profit over many years. Rather, the bridge loan would be immediately repaid in full upon the sale of the company's original building. This short-term loan would then have served its purpose by "bridging the gap" between the purchase of the bigger building and sale of the smaller one – mission accomplished.

The Ugliest Borrowing Need

A discussion of why businesses borrow wouldn't be complete without mentioning the least desirable reason of all: funding operating losses. All of the borrowing needs explained in the previous examples are very common and arise in the normal course of business for successful companies. But sometimes businesses struggle to survive due to sharp decreases in revenue or an unexpected spike in expenses. Perhaps a large percentage of the company's sales were to one customer, and now that customer has found a new vendor or gone out of business. Or maybe rising healthcare costs have made maintaining profitability impossible for the company. Whatever the cause of the company's deteriorating performance, it may approach its bank with a borrowing request to fund its operating losses until it can right the ship and repay the loan.

As you might imagine, banks are hesitant to lend to businesses for this reason. I told you in Chapter 1 that banks are in the business of managing risk, so lending money to a company running an unprofitable operation is far riskier than lending for capital expenditures or for working capital. Do banks ever lend to businesses that are losing money? Absolutely – in some instances it works out fine, and the bank gets repaid.

But this brings up a critical point I want to highlight, one that may not be as obvious as one would think: sometimes banks have to say "No." When companies approach a bank for a loan, even if the company has borrowed money from that bank before, it's not a "rubber stamp" approval. This highlights the importance of building those relationships I mentioned in the last chapter. You may know your customer so well that you can justify making the loan despite the company's poor current performance. Or if you do need to decline the loan request, the personal relationship you've built with the business owner may allow you to deliver the bad news diplomatically so you don't lose your customer.

Especially after the recent financial crisis in which a lot of banks suffered huge losses or went out of business, the need for banks to make sound credit decisions is more important than ever. This decision-making process is called underwriting, and I will cover it in detail in Chapter 3.

Before I close this review of why businesses borrow, I want to introduce a simple but profound fact. What do all of the borrowing needs and types of loans in this chapter have in common? In each case, the bank is always lending *cash*. Bakeries need raw materials and ovens, but banks never lend these items to its bakery customers. Auto manufacturers need coils of steel, but banks never lend steel to these companies. Banks lend cash and only cash to their borrowing customers. And the important corollary to this is that when borrowers want to repay their loans the only acceptable currency is cash.

In other words, the customer may have borrowed money to purchase an oven, but the bank never wants to be repaid with that oven (or any other collateral). Nor can the bank spend the customer's "market share" or "good reputation." These all have value to the customer, but the bank wants the borrower to use these assets to generate cash flow, which will in turn allow them to repay the bank. The importance of this simple truth will become more evident as we look at underwriting and structuring of loans in the following chapters.

Key Takeaways

Why Commercial Customers Borrow:

- **Capital Expenditures**
- **Real Estate Purchases**
- **Working Capital**
- **Start-ups**
- **Business Acquisitions**
- **Owner Buyouts**
- **Bridge Loans**
- **Funding Losses**

Remember: Only CASH Repays Loans!

Chapter 3

THE ART OF UNDERWRITING

Imagine you are a manufacturer living a few hundred years ago and wanting to ship a large quantity of goods from Europe to the new world. The risk of shipwreck was high, but you could make a fortune by getting those products safely across the Atlantic. Other businesses around you wanted to do the same but were also hesitant due to the possibility of losing everything.

The solution? All of you would approach an insurer, offering to pay him "premiums" for taking some of the risk in your venture. If your ship completed the voyage successfully, the insurer would keep your premium. If you weren't so fortunate, he would reimburse you for your loss, using the premiums he had collected from the others whose boats successfully made it to shore.

What about your neighbor who hired the drunken sea captain to guide his vessel and whose ship appeared anything but seaworthy? His boat may have never left the harbor because the insurer would have been unwilling to take a chance on him. Insurance, like banking, is risky business. So before accepting a premium and shaking hands on the deal, a wise insurer would have asked a lot of questions, interviewed the captain, and inspected that creaky old dinghy. If he concluded that the risk of loss outweighed the benefit of earning that premium, he would never have agreed to the deal.

As the story goes, insurers in these situations would list all known risks on one side of a piece of paper with the mitigating factors on the other side. If they were willing to accept the risks in exchange for a given premium, they would *write* their names *under* the list of risks – hence the term "underwriting." In commercial banking, the word refers to the process of deciding whether to lend money to a company after assessing the known risks.

As the title of this chapter suggests, underwriting is more of an art than a science. Banks spend millions of dollars each year hiring people to build sophisticated risk models, and these do serve a purpose. But ultimately the underwriting process is about finding a way to creatively craft a deal that makes sense for both the bank and the customer. It boils down to gathering sufficient information, using sound judgment, and being disciplined enough to say "No" when risks stray beyond a bank's pre-determined comfort zone.

One of the best senior credit officers I ever worked for was also a private pilot. He frequently compared the underwriting process to a pre-flight check. On his way to the airport he envisioned the fun of taking off and flying his plane. Yet when he got to his plane he would first painstakingly look for any and all reasons to stay on the ground. Why? He wanted to be aware of anything that could potentially go wrong. As with commercial lending, the best time to identify a problem is *before* you are airborne. Knowing what to expect and preparing to manage it makes for better lending and safer flying.

Every loan a bank makes carries some risk, and your job as a credit professional is to help your bank make smart underwriting decisions. This process is relatively quick and straightforward when an individual applies for a car loan in retail banking. The bank runs a personal credit report, and if the applicant's personal credit rating (FICO score) is good enough, the loan is approved. This entire process, which you may have witnessed the last time you bought a car at a dealership, takes about thirty minutes. But when the loan amount is $20,000,000 instead of $20,000 and the borrower is a company instead of an individual, the process is a bit more involved.

My overview of loan underwriting would be incomplete without first introducing you to the "5 C's of Credit." This helpful tool has been used for generations to remind credit professionals of the five most important factors to consider when lending money:

- Conditions
- Character
- Capital
- Capacity
- Collateral

I will explain the first four of these later in this chapter, and collateral will be covered in Chapter 4.

Before we begin looking at how commercial loans are underwritten, consider a more familiar scenario. Have you ever had a friend ask you to borrow ten dollars? If so, you probably made your decision within three seconds, and the "underwriting" process happened so quickly that you may not have been consciously aware of it. In short, you knew he would repay you within a few days, and if he didn't, you would be willing to accept the loss of your principal. Friends are friends, and $10 won't sink anyone, so you make the loan.

But what if a friend approached you and asked to borrow $1,000? Would your decision-making process change because of those two extra zeros? You bet it would (no pun intended). Assuming that you had $1,000 available to lend, questions would quickly pop into your mind, and you would be wise to seek acceptable answers.

What For?

You shouldn't accept a generic response like, "Because I'm broke," or, "It never hurts to have more." Worst of all would be, "I don't really know why I need to borrow the money. I seem to make enough, yet I always seem to be in need of more, and this time it's worse than usual." You would like to hear a specific, clear explanation of why your friend wants to borrow. "I just found the fishing boat of my dreams, and I'm afraid if I don't buy it today, it will be sold to someone else by tomorrow." You may not share your friend's enthusiasm about the boat, but at least the borrowing request makes sense.

Will You Pay Me Now or Pay Me Later?

In the $10 example, your decision was easy because you assumed you would be repaid quickly. You would have no "opportunity cost" because your $10 would be back in your pocket long before you might need it for something else. Understanding that larger loans often require longer repayment periods, you should follow your instincts that rightly tell you that your risk of not being repaid increases as this repayment period gets longer.

What's Your Plan?

Assuming that the borrowing need makes sense and you are comfortable with the length of the repayment terms, your next question might be, "How do you plan to pay me back?" That is, you would want to know where the money will come from.

Bankers call this the "primary source of repayment" (PSOR). In my boat example, a good answer might be, "My jet ski is for sale, and as soon as I sell it, I will pay you back." This plan isn't foolproof, but it's much better than, "I'm playing the lottery and feeling lucky" or even, "I'm in line for a big raise soon." The clearer and more predictable the source of repayment is, the better.

The Best-Laid Plans...

Good underwriters know that things don't always go according to plan. Before you write that $1,000 check, you should at least consider the possibility that the jet ski won't sell. Assuming you want your money back as soon as possible, you need to ask yourself a tougher question: what if your friend's repayment plan doesn't work out? Bankers refer to this as a "secondary source of repayment," and yours might sound something like, "I've always wanted a jet ski." I'll discuss this concept of securing a loan with collateral in Chapter 4.

Long-Distance Relationships

Here is a question that's not as obvious but one you should certainly consider: where does your friend live? In some cases, this might not matter, but the dynamics can be very different when you see your friend every day versus if he lives in another state. In a worst-case scenario, imagine trying to collect your money if your friend has turned against you or just stopped returning your phone calls. This would pose a much greater problem if you can't easily meet him face-to-face – especially if his jet ski is in *his* garage. Bankers call this lending "out of market," and it clearly poses additional risk.

His Word Is His Bond

All of these questions are important and ought to be asked. But the most critical factor to consider when making your decision might well be your friend's character. When all is said and done, will he

be good for it? This question again highlights the relational aspect of lending and underscores the importance of knowing whom you are doing business with. It also points

back to what I stated earlier: Underwriting is an art more than a science. It requires wisdom and sound judgment as much as an understanding of accounting and finance.

Now that you understand what the word "underwriting" means and you know how the thought process works, let's talk about the actual components of underwriting commercial loans. The factors to consider when deciding whether to lend money to a company fall into two broad categories: *qualitative* and *quantitative*. I will devote the remainder of this chapter to helping you understand the meaning and importance of these two categories.

Qualitative Analysis

If you tell your friends and family that you want to be a commercial banker and you will enter the field by working as an Underwriter or Credit Analyst, they will most likely assume you will be spending your office hours crunching numbers. After all, if a bank is going to lend millions of dollars to a business and it's your job to be sure they're doing it safely, then wouldn't you want to jump right into financial analysis? Not so fast. Before you even glance at the prospective borrower's financial statements, you must answer some basic questions first.

Industry Considerations

First, you want to understand something about the *industry* in which the business operates so that you can formulate an opinion about its viability. For example, Blockbuster Video opened its doors in 1985, and by 2004 its annual revenues peaked at almost $6 billion. (Interestingly, in 2000 Blockbuster had declined an opportunity to purchase a fledgling competitor called Netflix for only $50 million.) In 2004 when Blockbuster had 60,000 employees and 9,000 stores, it looked like a safe underwriting risk, and I'm sure bankers were lined up offering money to this wildly successful company. By 2010, however, Blockbuster had filed for bankruptcy, and willing lenders were scarce.

This is an extreme example of changing industry dynamics, but it shows the importance of knowing the nuances of the industry into which you are lending. Home entertainment was still booming in 2010, but technology changed how consumers accessed it. And the banks that were still lending money to Blockbuster as the industry abandoned its retail store model undoubtedly lost money on failed loans because they didn't foresee the impact of those changes.

Conversely, industries like energy exploration and health care are growing rapidly today, and banks that acquire industry expertise in areas like these are well positioned to profit from that growth. Within each of these industries are different sectors, some of which are riskier to lend to than others. For example, energy lending includes financing oil drilling, natural gas exploration, and coal mining; health care lending encompasses financing medical practices, hospitals, and nursing homes. But overall, banks will fare better lending into these growth markets than to video rental stores or fax machine manufacturers.

The Business Life Cycle

A second consideration in your qualitative analysis of a company is how far it has progressed in its business life. This figure illustrates how revenue levels vary over time as businesses move through these stages. Generally speaking, lending to companies in the *research and* 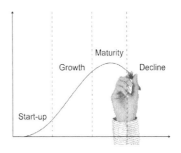 *development* or *start-up* phases is risky because these businesses are not yet generating much revenue. It's hard to make loan payments when no money is coming into your enterprise. Companies in high *growth* mode have larger revenues but are still at risk because of the greater cash requirements to buy inventory and finance accounts receivable. The sweet spot for banks is lending to *mature* companies because they typically generate good cash flow and have proven their viability. Many businesses remain in the mature stage for generations. Those that do slip into the stage of *declining* revenues pose an elevated risk to lenders. Their industry may be changing, a large customer may have been lost, or a new management team may be executing poorly. Whatever the reason for the decline, businesses in this stage often struggle with weaker cash flow, spelling bad news for their creditors.

Quality of Management

A Senior Vice President where I once worked offered this maxim for commercial lenders: "Bet on the jockey, not on the horse." What he meant is that products and business models are important

 to a company's success, but not as important as the quality of its management. In smaller companies, this might mean the owner whose entrepreneurial drive and vision keep

things moving in the right direction. In larger organizations, it could refer to an entire team of people that knows its industry, has solid relationships with its customers and suppliers, and is experienced in working through problems and economic cycles.

You won't have to be in commercial banking long to see a company ruined by a lack of a strong management succession plan. Dad starts the company with a creative idea, long hours, sound money management, and an entrepreneurial spirit. But one generation later when his son takes over running the company, Dad sadly watches as his son runs the company into the ground due to lack of experience or poor financial decisions.

The key point for you to grasp as a new banker is this: a terrific company with mediocre management may soon be in trouble, but an average business led by talented and experienced people will eventually thrive. Remember that banking is about relationships, and you will do well if you invest time getting to know the people who run the companies to whom you lend money.

One last word about management quality: beware of doing business with people you don't trust. Many of banks' biggest credit losses are the result of dishonesty or outright fraud on the part of borrowers. If you have an interaction with a borrower and something doesn't feel right, trust your instincts and part company. Character matters, especially when it comes to lending large sums of money.

Crunch Those Numbers – Quantitative Analysis

Congratulations! Now you understand a bit of the art of underwriting, and you know that it begins with doing some qualitative analysis: evaluating your borrower's industry, life cycle stage, and quality of management. You are now ready to tackle the other half of the underwriting equation – crunching the numbers, which is known as "quantitative analysis." Remember that underwriting is the process of deciding whether to lend money to a borrower. Assuming that the qualitative factors look acceptable, now you want to get a clear picture of the company's financial position and performance. In other words, you want to analyze the company's balance sheet (financial position) and income statement (financial performance) to determine if you think the company is creditworthy.

For a more detailed look at quantitative analysis, invest in the full online course at BreakingIntoBanking.com

---

Balance Sheet Analysis

Have you ever heard people say they are "property rich and cash poor?" This means they have assets (in this case, real estate) that are worth something, but they still can't put their hands on enough cash to pay their bills. They could sell their real estate to generate cash, but they either can't or don't want to do so. This is a *liquidity* problem, where liquidity is defined as "the ability to convert an asset to cash with little or no loss in value."

Companies can suffer from the same malady. They have often invested most of their cash into buildings, vehicles, and inventory, so when things get tight and the company needs cash, it's hard to come by. Why do bankers care about this? Because we lend cash and want to be repaid in cash. If our borrowers struggle with weak liquidity, then our risk of not being repaid (default risk) increases.

The other key financial metric on a company's balance sheet, *leverage*, can be illustrated by thinking about the value your home. Let's say you bought your home four years ago for $100,000, using $20,000 of your savings as a down payment and borrowing the remaining $80,000. You used leverage to buy the home – putting a little of your own money at risk and asking the bank to put *more* of its capital at risk. You then owned a home worth $100,000, financed by $80,000 *debt* and $20,000 *equity*. Your leverage would be expressed as a ratio of debt to equity, in this case 80,000/20,000 or 4:1 (four times). Another way to look at this is that the bank had 80% ownership of your home and you had 20%.

Now, four years later, you have paid the loan balance down to $75,000, and your home is still worth $100,000, so your equity has increased to $25,000 and your debt has decreased to $75,000. Your leverage ratio is now 75,000 / 25,000 or 3:1. Essentially you now own a greater percentage of your home than you did a few years ago.

What's the point of the leverage discussion? Most of us use financial leverage to borrow money with a goal of decreasing our leverage over time. Similarly, your bank agreed to lend you money at a leverage ratio of 4:1 because they expected you to pay the balance down over time, thus decreasing *their* risk. Banks want their borrowers to have *some* leverage – if no one is borrowing, banks go out of business. But many banks learned a painful lesson in 2008: if you allow people to borrow 95% of the value of their homes (leverage ratio of 19:1), bad things can happen for both bank and borrower.

The same rules apply in commercial lending. Banks want their customers to borrow money so that they can earn interest rate spread and fee income. But how much should a bank lend to its customer? How much debt is too much? Just as in our homeowner example, a company's financial leverage can be easily measured by examining its balance sheet and calculating the ratio of its debt to equity. My goal here isn't to walk you through those calculations. Rather, I want you to understand *why* leverage is important: it shows you how much risk the borrower is willing to take versus how much risk the bank is taking. I told you in Chapter 1 that banks are in the business of risk management. Understanding a company's leverage is one of the best ways for a bank to measure and manage the risk of lending money to that company.

Income Statement Analysis

Just as a company's balance sheet provides clues about its credit risk, its income statement is also a wealth of information for those who know how to read it. By learning to analyze revenue trends, profit margins, and a company's sustainable cash flow, you will be well prepared to decide whether to lend that company money. In my Introduction, I promised you this book would not be a credit training manual but rather a peek into what commercial credit professionals actually do. But since it's helpful to see some concrete examples, I will briefly explain two common income statement ratios and their importance as I did with balance sheet analysis.

Debt Service and Fixed Charge Coverage

Imagine you are considering making a commercial loan to a company with the total annual principal and interest payments (debt service) on the loan totaling $200,000. If your calculations told you the company generated enough profit to have $180,000 available annually to repay (service) the debt, would you be comfortable making the loan? Hopefully not – you would want the company to have at least $200,000 available for debt service. This would yield a "debt service coverage" (DSC) ratio of 1:1, indicating that the company could make its required payments with nothing left over.

But do businesses use their profits for anything other than debt repayment? Try to answer this question by putting yourself into the shoes of the business owner. After all operating expenses are paid and you have taken your salary, what would you want to do with your profits? First, you would pay your income taxes. Then, perhaps you would reinvest into your company – purchasing new manufacturing equipment or delivery trucks so that you can service more customers. And what about that vacation home you have been dreaming of ever since you started your business years ago?

The point of these questions is that businesses use their profits for more than just debt service, so when you analyze a company's cash flow, you need to account for all of these other needs, which bankers refer to as "fixed charges." Your job as a Credit Analyst will be to determine your borrower's capacity to pay for (cover) these fixed charges out of its available cash flow. This capacity is measured by a company's "fixed charge coverage" (FCC) ratio, and mastering this concept will be critical to your success in commercial banking.

Summary

The art of underwriting takes years to master, and you are starting on solid ground by understanding the key points in this chapter. Asking thoughtful questions and looking for risks is essential, but ultimately good underwriting results in discovering ways to make loans to customers whenever possible. Learning to strike this balance between risk management and business development will make you a valuable asset to your bank. Frequently your underwriting will lead you to decide "Yes" on a loan request even though risks are inherent in the transaction. How will you manage those risks? This question is answered in the next chapter on Loan Structuring.

The 5 C's of Credit

Conditions:	Qualitative factors impacting a borrower's financial performance Do the borrower's non-financial indicators predict success?
Character:	Borrower's intent and willingness to honor the loan agreement Do you trust your borrower?
Capital:	Borrower's equity or willingness to share in the risk Does the borrower have "skin in the game?"
Capacity:	Sufficiency of borrower's cash flow to service its obligations Are the borrower's coverage ratios acceptable?
Collateral:	Bank's backup plan if borrower cannot repay its loan Will the borrower pledge its assets to make the bank whole?

ANDY KEUSAL

Chapter 4

LOAN STRUCTURING:

IMPROVING YOUR ODDS

Generations ago, banks loaned money on a handshake and a promise to repay. Character was king, so a rigorous underwriting process was not really necessary. If a company wanted to borrow money, the owner gave his word to the bank that the money would be repaid as agreed, knowing that his good name would be ruined if his promise wasn't kept.

Today, things are a bit more complicated. Competition among banks is fierce, so profit margins are thin, and banks can't afford many lending mistakes. Even if banks wanted to lend more freely and give their borrowers more latitude, banking regulators would never allow it. The result, as you learned in the last chapter, is that banks must now underwrite thoroughly and thoughtfully before making a commercial loan.

Even after all pertinent qualitative and quantitative factors have been considered and a bank decides to lend money to a business, one important step remains: the loan must be properly *structured*. This means the loan should have characteristics appropriate to the borrowing purpose. These characteristics (structural elements) include:

- Type of loan
- Repayment period
- Pricing
- Risk mitigants

This chapter will cover each of these elements, including definitions, purposes, and examples of each.

Facility Types

I confessed in my Introduction that my banking career did not start well and I wanted to help you avoid the mistakes I made. Imagine my embarrassment when, after almost a month on the job, I learned that in commercial banking a "facility" refers to a loan, not to a building. Finally I understood why a small company would need *four* different facilities!

Having spared you similar embarrassment, let me remind you of what I explained in Chapter 2 – that businesses borrow for different reasons, and each borrowing purpose dictates a unique type of facility:

- Lines of credit for seasonal or short-term working capital financing
- Term loans for capital expenditures, business acquisitions, or buy-outs
- Mortgage loans for purchasing real estate
- Construction loans to finance new building projects
- Bridge loans to fill a short-term gap until a liquidity event happens
- Time notes, term loans, or lines of credit to finance operating losses

This list is not exhaustive, but it points out that facility types are not "one size fits all" although all of them involve money being lent from bank to borrower. Each facility type is like a tool in your tool belt, and you must learn which one to reach for in any given situation.

Tenor and Amortization

These words may be unfamiliar to you, but we have already alluded to them when discussing the duration of a loan. *Tenor* refers to how long it takes a loan to mature, or come due for full payment. *Amortization* tells us over what period of time the principal amount of the loan will be paid back.

In some cases, the tenor and the amortization period are the same. For example, consider a company that borrows money to buy a new piece of equipment with an expected useful life of five years. The machine will generate increased profitability for the business for at least five years, so allowing the company five years to pay off the loan would be reasonable, with the additional profits serving as the source of repayment. In the 60th month of the loan, the final monthly payment would be made, and the loan would be paid off concurrent with its maturity.

Contrast this with a real estate mortgage loan, which we would *not* expect to be repaid in five years, given the higher price tag and longer useful life of the building. A 25-year amortization (repayment schedule) would be more appropriate and would result in a much lower monthly payment for the borrower. The tenor, however, might still be only five years. This means the loan would mature after only five years with a balloon payment (the remaining principal balance) being due at that time. In essence, the bank is then putting its money at risk for only five years instead of twenty-five. In many cases, if the bank is still comfortable with the risk, the borrower will refinance the remaining balance by extending the maturity date for another five years. This type of 5-year tenor/ 25-year amortization facility is very common, and it highlights the difference between a loan *maturing* and it being *paid off.*

Pricing

I explained in Chapter 1 how banks make money from interest rate spread. The interest rate the bank charges the borrower is clearly one of the most important structural elements of the loan. But how do banks decide what a loan's interest rate should be?

Theoretically, loan pricing is based on risk – the greater the risk, the higher the interest rate spread should be. Many banks have even built complex pricing models that dictate spreads based on various specified risk factors. This is another example of "quid pro quo" –

if banks are willing to take additional risk, they should be compensated for doing so by earning higher margins. This "risk/reward" concept, however, is true only up to a point. Some borrowers simply pose too much risk, and no interest rate spread can adequately compensate the bank for it. In these cases, disciplined banks should simply say "No" and walk away.

I stated that pricing is theoretically tied to risk, but theory doesn't always correlate to reality. If the underwriting process leads a bank to believe that a prospective borrower is a good credit risk, then structural elements, especially pricing, are frequently compromised due to competitive pressure. For example, the risk profile of a borrower may suggest a spread of 250 bps (the bank's cost of funds plus 2.50%), but if the bank wants to win the business badly enough from a rival institution, it may lower its spread to 175 bps. Although this strategy results in a lower profit margin for the bank, it's safer than those loans structured with bigger spreads to compensate for exceptionally high risk.

All of the elements I have explained so far are spelled out in a document called a "promissory note." This note includes the legal names of the bank and the borrower, the amount of the loan, how it is to be repaid, and the interest rate. It is signed by both parties, and in some cases, this simple document is all that is required to close a commercial loan. The bank promises to lend the funds, the borrower promises to repay, and the deal is done. In most instances, however, the transaction is more complex and also requires a written "loan agreement" that details additional structural elements (risk mitigants) of the loan.

Mitigating Risk

Remember that underwriting a loan request is not about deciding whether or not the request carries risk; all loans have some degree of risk. It is about measuring and understanding the risk, then structuring the loan accordingly. So once you have selected an appropriate facility type, matched its tenor and amortization to its purpose, and priced it appropriately, it's time to think about how to *mitigate* (lessen) the risks identified in the underwriting process. The three primary tools commercial bankers use for this are:

- *Collateral*
- *Loan covenants*
- *Guarantees*

Before I explain each of these three tools, I want to remind you of what I said at the end of Chapter 2: only *cash* repays loans. As helpful as collateral, loan covenants, and guarantees are, none of them can repay a loan. Generally, banks underwrite loan requests to determine if the borrower's cash flow will be sufficient to make the required loan payments. The three risk mitigation tools discussed here are meaningful supports when cash flow dries up, but they are not primary sources of repayment. Remembering and applying this simple truth will put the following discussion into the proper context and will make you a better banker.

Collateral

I had terrific parents who worked hard to teach me life's important lessons, but I also picked up some key learning from watching "The Brady Bunch" on television. In one episode, two of the Brady children approached the local banker to borrow money to buy an anniversary gift for their parents and were asked what they had to offer as collateral. Bobby Brady asked what collateral was and was told by the friendly banker that it was something of real value like real estate, jewelry, stocks, and bonds you had to pledge if you wanted to get a loan. The Brady boy's natural response was, "If we had all that stuff, we wouldn't need the loan!"

This scene serves to remind us that good commercial bankers must be skeptics. When we build a relationship with a new borrower, underwrite their credit risk, and decide to lend them money, we believe they will repay us. But it's a good idea to have a backup plan...just in case. Even when our quantitative analysis tells us that our borrower will generate sufficient cash flow to make the required loan payments, we still sleep better at night knowing that we have a Plan B if their cash flow dries up. Bankers refer to this backup plan as a "secondary source of repayment."

Usually that plan includes "securing" the loan with something of value – collateral – that we have the right to liquidate if necessary to get our money back. If you have ever borrowed money to buy a car or a home, you have pledged those assets as collateral for those loans. You don't own the asset "free and clear" (of liens) until you pay off the loan and receive the title or deed in the mail stamped "Paid in Full." Similarly, collateral for a commercial loan can be any asset the company is willing to pledge, including equipment, vehicles, real estate, inventory, accounts receivable, or even cash. Often, collateral is simply stated as "all business assets."

Since collateral is such a fundamental component of risk mitigation, I want to drill a little deeper on this subject. As you read about each element of loan structure, think again about your friend who wants to borrow $1,000 from you – this approach will allow these abstract concepts to crystalize more vividly in your mind. Remember his jet ski? If he agreed to pledge it as collateral, do you have that pledge in writing? Where is the jet ski, and how easy would it be for you to get it? Would you need him to sign over the title to you before it would legally be yours? You can see from these questions that securing a loan with collateral is not as simple as it first appears.

Consider the following characteristics of your collateral:

- Location
  - ➤ Do you know where it is?
  - ➤ Is it all in one place or scattered in various known or unknown places?
  - ➤ How much would it cost you to find it, collect it, and sell it?
- Liquidity
  - ➤ How quickly and simply could you convert it to cash?
  - ➤ Is it "self-liquidating" (e.g., inventory) or not (e.g., real estate)?
  - ➤ How much would you actually get for it if sold at auction?
- Marketability
  - ➤ Would the bank be able to sell it if your borrower couldn't?
  - ➤ Is the bank legally allowed to liquidate it (e.g., alcohol, firearms)?

- Public Relations
  - ➢ Would the bank sustain reputational damage by liquidating it?
  - ➢ Would the bank foreclose on a church or university?

Generally speaking, banks like to secure loans with as much collateral as possible despite some of the limitations mentioned here. Remember that taking collateral doesn't mean that the bank physically holds the assets; it simply means that the bank has the right to seize and sell those assets if the borrower defaults on the loan.

Infrequently, when a borrower is deemed to be extremely creditworthy, banks will lend money on an "unsecured" basis – with no collateral pledged at all. This is typically done only when the borrower is a large, mature company with very stable earnings and a rock-solid balance sheet.

Loan Covenants

The word *covenant* simply means an agreement between two parties. In commercial banking, a loan covenant refers to a written agreement between the bank and the borrower in which the borrower promises to do (affirmative) or not do (negative) certain things. These covenants can also be financial or non-financial. I have provided one example of each type of covenant in the following box.

Affirmative Financial	Borrower must maintain minimum net worth of $1,000,000
Affirmative Non-Financial	Borrower must provide financial statements quarterly
Negative Financial	Borrower's debt service coverage must not be < 1.25:1
Negative Non-Financial	Borrower cannot change ownership without bank consent

Loan covenants are meant to act as guardrails between which the borrower may safely drive. If they swerve beyond these boundaries, they are said to have "tripped" or "breached" the covenant. This is serious business because the borrower has broken its promise *even if it has continued to make its required loan payments*. Failure to comply with a loan covenant is considered an event of default. This means that the bank can call the loan, forcing the borrower to pay the full balance immediately. In practice, banks rarely do this, but it does allow them to renegotiate the pricing on the loan or charge a fee for waiving the covenant default.

Covenants are a valuable tool for banks, but they don't repay loans. Remember the cardinal rule of lending: banks lend only cash, and only cash can repay a loan. Collateral provides a backup plan, and covenants allow bankers to keep their fingers on the pulse of their borrowers, but neither of these tools can repay a loan.

Guarantees

As a boy, I was blessed to have a number of entrepreneurial relatives. When I was a teenager and my uncle was in his fifties, he had an opportunity to buy a business for $1.5 million. He had done his homework, believing he could improve the company's operations and increase its profitability, making it a sound investment. The only problem was that he was about $1.25 million short. So he formed a corporation and approached a bank to borrow the necessary funds under the name of his new business.

The underwriters believed in my uncle's business plan and were willing to lend money to his company but required that he *personally guarantee* the debt. As I sat at their dining room table one evening listening to him explain this scenario to my aunt, she asked the very question I was thinking: what is a personal guarantee? My uncle explained that if he guaranteed the loan and his business was not able to make the loan payments, the bank would have the right (recourse) to come directly to my uncle and demand the payments from him. Where collateral is a secondary source of repayment, guarantees are a third ("tertiary") source.

Needless to say, my uncle and aunt thought long and hard before they decided to sign that guarantee. My uncle was putting his house and life savings at risk, but he believed his business would succeed and was willing to share in some of the risk along with the bank. From an underwriting standpoint, the bank knew that my uncle didn't have enough personal assets to repay the entire loan. But by having his personal guarantee, the bank made certain that he was completely emotionally committed to his company's success – he had "skin in the game." Ultimately, the business was very successful, and the loan was repaid as agreed. The bank had offloaded some of its risk to its borrower, and the guarantee had served its purpose. And my uncle got to retire comfortably in a warmer climate.

A parent company can also provide a guarantee to its subsidiary. These are called "corporate guarantees" versus personal guarantees in my earlier example. In either case, sometimes the guarantee is not for the full amount of the loan, but for a limited dollar amount or percentage of the outstanding balance only. These "limited guarantees" serve as a compromise when banks want a full (unlimited) guarantee but the borrower is unwilling to take that much risk. Loans made with no guarantees of any kind are called "non-recourse."

Let's Make a Deal

Now that you are familiar with the structural elements of a commercial loan, you may be wondering how the bank actually puts these pieces together on any particular loan. If you were the underwriter or Credit Analyst and were seeking to minimize the bank's credit risk, you would want to structure every loan as follows:

- Big interest rate spread and plenty of fees
- Fully secured with all available collateral
- Numerous loan covenants to set clear expectations with your borrower
- Full personal or corporate guarantee

Now put yourself in the customer's shoes. If you were the owner or CFO of a company, you would want to borrow money under these conditions:

- Low interest rate with no fees
- Not pledging any of your company's assets as collateral
- No covenants to constrain financial or management decisions
- Minimize additional risk by avoiding guarantees

In other words, banks want as tight of a structure as possible, and borrowers want the exact opposite. So who decides? It's a  negotiation process. Your bank isn't the only game in town, and creditworthy businesses will be courted by many of your competitors. So the free market – competition – will result in structuring a deal that is acceptable to both bank and borrower. Some borrowers will gladly pledge additional collateral in exchange for lower pricing. Others would rather accept a higher interest rate if they can negotiate looser covenants or avoid signing a guarantee. The end product of this haggling is a loan agreement, signed by both parties, that specifies the collateral, covenants (if any), and any guarantor(s).

The Sixth "C"

Having introduced you to the Five C's of Credit, I'll end this chapter with an insider tip about the impact of the 6th "C" – Competition. Often, so many banks in the market are willing to lend capital that borrowers gain too much control in the negotiation. Banks wants to grow their assets (loan balances), so to win new business (or keep existing customers from leaving) they start offering overaggressive structures: loose covenants ("covenant lite"), non-recourse (no guarantees), and thin spreads (exception pricing).

In the short term, banks may make more loans, but these structural compromises often come back to haunt banks in the form of "problem loans." When borrowers have problems making their loan payments, their banks have little to fall back on, so they end up charging off unpaid balances and losing money on these loans. I'll talk more about this in Chapter 6 when we look at risk grades. For now, keep in mind that the best time for banks to negotiate for collateral, covenants, and guarantees is *before* a loan is made when the borrower needs the bank's money. Once the loan is approved and funded, the customer will be far less likely to provide additional structural considerations.

The <u>6</u> C's of Credit

Conditions:	Qualitative factors impacting a borrower's financial performance Do the borrower's non-financial indicators predict success?
Character:	Borrower's intent and willingness to honor the loan agreement Do you trust your borrower?
Capital:	Borrower's equity or willingness to share in the risk Does the borrower have "skin in the game?"
Capacity:	Sufficiency of borrower's cash flow to service its obligations Are the borrower's coverage ratios acceptable?
Collateral:	Bank's backup plan if borrower cannot repay its loan Will the borrower pledge its assets to make the bank whole?
Competition:	Banks must be disciplined and guard against overaggressive structure What are other banks in the market offering to customers?

Key Takeaways

Structural Tools to Mitigate Risk:

- **Collateral**
- **Loan Covenants**
- **Guarantees**

ANDY KEUSAL

Chapter 5

GETTING THE "THUMBS UP" –

THE CREDIT APPROVAL PROCESS

Before I help you understand the process of getting a loan approved, I want to pause and say, "Well done!" for getting this far. The last few chapters were packed with a lot of ideas and terms that might be new to you. Don't worry about mastering them or knowing how to apply what you have learned right now. Remember that the objective of this book is simply to introduce you to the most important pieces of the  banking puzzle and to show you that they do indeed fit together. As the subtitle of my book suggests, learning all of this feels at first like cracking the code on a safe, but it won't seem so mysterious once you have turned the book's last page.

This short chapter is about the chronological flow of getting a loan approved. This process varies based on whether you work for a large institution or a small community bank, but the flow is generally the same regardless of where you work. Someone in the bank must approve all loan requests before the customer gets any money, so let's talk about how that happens.

I told you in Chapter 1 that banking is about building relationships. If you are married, you have probably reminisced many times about how you met your spouse, got to know one another, learned one another's strengths and weaknesses, and ultimately committed to each other. Commercial banking relationships aren't nearly as fun or romantic, but they do progress through similar phases.

When Harry Met Sally

All banking relationships start with an introduction. Your bank may have become acquainted with a customer through a personal meeting or by a referral from an accounting firm or an attorney. The company may have become disgruntled with its current bank, or perhaps the business simply outgrew its bank's capabilities. When a company starts looking for a new bank, whatever the reason, a "courtship" begins that can last anywhere from a few weeks to many years. It can be very inconvenient for a business to move its accounts, cash management services, and loans from one bank to another, so it happens only when there is a good reason to do so.

Because commercial banking is so relationship-driven, having a new banker assigned to manage a company's relationship is often the trigger for changing banks. That is, a company will spend years "educating" a banker (also called "Lender" or "Relationship Manager") about its market, its needs, and its niche in an industry. When that banker retires or takes a new position, businesses sometimes feel betrayed and frustrated; now they have to start all over, helping their new Relationship Manager get up to speed on their business. This creates a ripe opportunity for competing banks courting the company to move in and win that company's banking relationship.

You already know what happens next in the process. The new bank, perhaps the one you work for, collects the company's financial statements for the past three years, and the underwriting process begins. If you work for a large bank, a team of people, including Credit Analysts, underwriters, senior credit officers, and the Relationship Manager, may do the underwriting. In smaller shops, you may be the one doing all of the qualitative and quantitative work yourself, partnering with the banker to reach a conclusion.

Piecing It Together

In either case, the underwriting process quickly begins to overlap with loan structuring. I walked you through Chapters 3 and 4 sequentially, but in reality the underwriting and the structuring of a loan happen somewhat concurrently. For example, if your  underwriting analysis suggests that you are heading toward a positive decision, then you immediately begin thinking about what the elements of the loan would look like. If your quantitative analysis reveals that the borrower has weak cash flow, your structure would likely include a covenant related to cash flow. If the company doesn't have much capital, your structure might require the personal guarantee of the company's owner. Your thought process would sound like, "We can approve a loan to this borrower, but it would have to include these specific structural elements."

The tricky part here is that bankers actually have to negotiate and "sell" the deal they have structured to two different parties. They must protect the interest of the bank by negotiating as tight of a structure as possible while still making it acceptable to the borrower. In the last chapter, I explained how the bank wants lots of collateral, tight loan covenants, and a guarantee. The customer, on the other hand, wants to offer none of those things. Good bankers must be able to strike a balance and keep both sides happy. As you can see, this requires years of experience along with attention to detail and strong interpersonal skills.

May I Have Your Autograph?

Once a loan has been structured that is acceptable to both bank and borrower, the bank needs to officially approve the loan request as it is written in the loan agreement. Some banks have one designated person, usually a senior credit officer, who has the "power of the pen" – the authority to approve lending the money to the borrower. In other banks, a committee consisting of senior credit officers, lending managers, and occasionally even the bank president makes the decision. The idea behind the committee approval process is that there is wisdom in having various perspectives at the table, thus minimizing the chances of critical questions not getting answered.

When I was a new Credit Analyst and someone explained this process to me, I was concerned that my lack of experience would lead to my making bad underwriting decisions, costing the bank money (and costing me my job). I soon learned that I wouldn't have the power of that pen until I had the knowledge and experience to use it, so the pressure was off, at least for a while. Your input will be valued, and you certainly play an important part in the process. Those with credit authority are counting on you to provide them with accurate information so their decisions can be sound. But no one will expect you to make the final call until you have more experience under your belt.

The Documents

One of the things you will spend a lot of time on during the credit approval process is *writing*. You may not have thought of commercial banking as a writing job, but it is, especially when you are working in the credit function. Much of the underwriting and structuring may initially be informal conversations, but soon into the process you will need to document those discussions in writing. To excel in this part of your job, you will need strong organizational and business writing skills as well as being attentive to detail. I have managed many people who quickly grasped the accounting and financial aspects of the job but who struggled to organize their thoughts and put them on paper. If you have room to improve in this area, see my Recommended Resources on page 149.

Most banks use some type of template to summarize all of the pertinent information needed to make a credit decision. The end result of the underwriting and structuring process is a document that contains:

- The borrower's legal name, address, and company background
- A summary of how much credit exposure the bank would have to the borrower if the loan(s) were approved
- The types of loan facilities being requested and the dollar amount of each

- The borrower's risk rating and classification (more on this in chapter 6)
- Your written narrative highlighting the risks associated with lending to this borrower and your proposed structure to mitigate those risks

If the appropriate person or committee approves the request, they sign and date it, acknowledging that the bank is prepared to lend the money. The signed credit package is then sent to a loan closer (also known as document preparer or doc prep) who prepares the legal documents that the bank and borrower will sign at the loan closing. These documents include the promissory note and the loan agreement, both of which I described in Chapter 4. If all goes well at the closing, the documents get signed, and the bank disburses funds to the borrower. In my marriage analogy, this is like the wedding day. Everyone is happy: the customer receives the money it needs, the bank adds another income-producing asset to its balance sheet, and you enjoy the satisfaction of knowing that you had a hand in making it happen.

Left at the Altar

But not all of the deals you work on will have such a happy ending. You will frequently labor for weeks writing a credit package only to have someone in the bank decide they aren't comfortable with the risk. Perhaps the exposure amount was deemed too high for a company in a given industry. Or maybe some details came to light during the underwriting process that raised concerns about the quality of the company's management or its capacity to service the debt being requested. In some cases, the prospective customer decides to borrow from another bank because its price or structure was more agreeable. For whatever reason, sometimes your work ends up in a "dead deal." This can be frustrating and disappointing because you have invested so much time and energy into it, but you can't take it personally – it's all part of the job.

The entire process from introduction to loan closing can take as little as a few weeks to as long as a few years. It depends on how eager the customer is to switch banks, how willing the bank is to lend to the customer, and how many other credit requests are in the bank's pipeline. And once the loan is closed, that's not the end of the story. Like any good marriage, the wedding day is just the beginning. Now the bank begins its process of monitoring and reporting on the relationship, which I will explain in Chapter 6.

Credit Approval Process Flow Chart

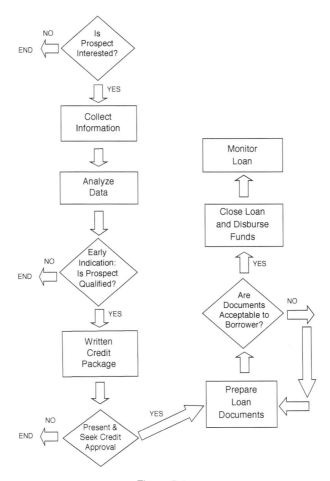

Figure 5.1

ANDY KEUSAL

Chapter 6

SHIFTING TO MONITORING MODE

Having read this far, you now know that commercial lending is significantly different than consumer lending. When you are approved for a car loan, you typically sign a few papers, drive your new wheels off the car lot, and begin making monthly payments for the next five years until your loan is paid off. The bank or auto finance company that loaned you the money underwrote your risk and let you borrow the money. They have made millions of these types of loans, and they recognize that a small percentage of borrowers don't make their required payments on time. Those who fall far enough behind have their cars repossessed.

But as long as you make your monthly payments as agreed, that bank won't be calling you a year later to ask for your tax return or a copy of your most recent paycheck. In other words, after doing their initial underwriting at the time of your loan request, you never hear from them again. Five years later, that glorious day comes when you make your last payment, and they send you the original title to your automobile with a copy of your loan paperwork stamped, "Paid In Full."

As you have probably already guessed, the scenario described above does not apply to commercial loans. Immediately after the funds are disbursed, banks begin the process of checking up on (monitoring) their borrowers. This wouldn't be practical in consumer lending because of the number of loans and the relatively small dollar amount of each loan. Where consumer lending is more transactional, commercial lending is more relationship-oriented, which means keeping in touch is paramount for both the bank and its customers.

So far in this book, I have focused my discussion on underwriting, structuring, and approving *new* loan requests. But a large part of what you will do daily pertains to the existing loans already made to your bank's current customers. This includes annual reviews, appraisals, field exams, and covenant compliance. I will explain each of these in more detail, and then I'll wrap up the chapter by showing you how a bank steps back and takes a broader look at its entire portfolio of loans.

Annual Reviews

I told you in Chapter 2 that I planted 27 fruit trees on the back half of my property a few years ago. As with most home improvement projects, it took more time, energy, and money than expected, but I eventually got those trees into the ground. After spending considerable money on tree stakes, organic fertilizer, and four hundred feet of garden hose, I was pretty committed to  keeping those trees alive and well. Because I had done the work to plant, feed, and water my young trees, I expected to eventually reap the fruit of my labor.

Though I didn't expect to see apples until years later, I still made regular trips to my orchard that first year. Why? I wanted to see first-hand how they were getting along. One thing I learned was that the deer in my woods had an equally intense interest in my fruit trees. This led me to invest in an additional level of protection that I hadn't thought of initially – five hundred feet of fencing around the perimeter of the orchard. The point is that a lot of bad things can happen in a short period of time, especially if you aren't paying close attention.

For this reason, most banks review each of their commercial relationships annually. Aside from satisfying regulatory requirements, this is also a sound risk management practice. It allows the bankers to reconnect with their customers and to get a sense of how things are going in the business. Specifically, an annual review should include:

- A face-to-face meeting between the banker(s) and the

management of the company, ideally at the customer's place of business

- The collection of current financial statements
- A review of any significant changes since the last meeting
- Creation of a written summary to document the review

Ideally, bankers should be in contact with their customers frequently throughout the year because waiting a year may be too late to remedy a deteriorating situation.

Here is one bit of advice that will pay huge dividends as you seek to learn and make a good impression in your first year: whenever a lender from your bank is going to meet with a bank customer, ask to go along. It's very common for a banker to make two or three in-person "customer calls" with each borrower during a given year, so there should be plenty of opportunities for you to join one of these meetings. You will come away from these meetings with a much better understanding of the customer's business, so your credit packages will be better. And you will enjoy your job more if you are out in the action instead of always being at your desk.

Appraisals

You know by now that banks frequently lend money to companies for fixed assets like equipment and real estate. You also know that those loans are usually secured by the fixed assets as collateral for the loan. For example, if a company wants to buy a building for $1,000,000, it might use $200,000 of its own capital for a down payment and borrow the remaining $800,000 from a bank. In these situations, the bank will have an independent professional real estate appraiser research the property and determine how much it is worth. If the appraiser says it's worth $1,000,000, then the deal makes sense, so the bank would be inclined to make the loan. But if the appraiser finds the value to be only $850,000, then the bank would only be willing to lend 80% of that value, or about $680,000. This appraisal process protects the bank if the property's value declines over the next few years.

Appraisals are also helpful tools when monitoring existing loans. If a bank made an $800,000 loan for a $1,000,000 building in Detroit in 2007, how much would that building be worth in 2011? Given what the decline in the automobile business did to property values in Detroit, it's fair to say that the building would probably be worth a lot less in 2011 than it was in 2007. But how much less? That property is your bank's collateral, so it's important that you understand its current value. Having it reappraised can give you that information.

This same process applies to appraising equipment. Just as some professional appraisers specialize in commercial real estate, others know the commercial equipment market inside and out. I'm not talking about small, inexpensive equipment like furniture and computers, but rather large, pricy items such as stamping machines, earthmoving vehicles, and forklifts.

Imagine that your bank made a loan four years ago, and now you are concerned that the value of your collateral, the equipment or property, has declined. After ordering an appraisal, you learn that your instincts were correct – the outstanding balance on the loan now exceeds the value of your collateral. Your secondary source of repayment, liquidation of collateral, is now in jeopardy. What should you do? You might ask your borrower to make an additional lump sum payment to "right-size" the loan. Or you could ask your customer to pledge something else as additional collateral. Are your borrowers required to do either of these? No. As long as they are making their payments and are in compliance with their loan covenants, they are under no obligation to help their banker sleep better at night. You can still ask, but how the customer responds will depend largely on the relationship you have built with them.

Field Exams

Appraisals are helpful tools to monitor the value of fixed assets as collateral. But what about when your collateral consists of working capital assets like accounts receivable and inventory? This is typically the case when your borrower has a working capital line of credit. As with fixed assets, you may want to check in periodically to determine the current value of this "self-liquidating" collateral. Is the company's inventory readily sellable, or is part of it now obsolete? Are all of the accounts receivable collectible, or are some of these IOUs stale and not likely to ever be received by your customer?

The simplest way to learn this is to conduct a "field exam" (collateral audit). This involves sending someone from the bank to spend a few days with your customer at their place of business, examining their accounts receivable and counting their inventory. This might sound intrusive, but it is a common practice among banks, so most businesses are accustomed to it. And assuming they have nothing to hide, they welcome the opportunity to confirm for their bank the quality of their working capital assets. In some cases, banks may wait years before conducting a collateral audit; with other customers, it may be done quarterly. Again, field exams can  sometimes cause friction between bank and customer, or they can be a routine part of business as usual, depending on the relationship that has been established. This is another instance where positive and proactive management of customer relationships can smooth a potentially bumpy situation.

Covenant Compliance

In Chapter 4, I explained that the purpose of loan covenants is to establish "guard rails" for the borrower when a loan is made. In doing this, the bank is setting expectations of its borrower's behaviors, and the loan isn't closed unless the customer understands these expectations, then agrees to abide by them.

 Naturally, the bank will want to monitor whether the borrower is complying with the agreed-upon covenants, and the frequency of this monitoring is spelled out in the loan agreement. It should be done at least annually, and most commonly covenants are tested quarterly.

Testing covenant compliance is one of the most important tasks you will do as a Credit Analyst. Once a new relationship is established and the loan is closed, Relationship Managers are encouraged to focus their energy and attention on winning new business – finding and courting new borrowing customers. The responsibility for monitoring existing borrowers' performance is left to you, and the importance of doing this well will be evident when we look at portfolio metrics later in this chapter.

The process consists of the following steps:

1. *Tracking receipt of the customer's financial statements.* The most basic requirement in any loan agreement is that the customer must submit fiscal year-end statements in a timely manner. It also often requires submission of year-to-date (interim) statements monthly or quarterly.
2. *Tracking receipt of the borrower's covenant compliance certificate.* This short document, created by the customer,

lists each covenant and shows whether the customer was in compliance as of the specified date. For example, it might read:

> a. Borrower to maintain minimum Net Worth of $500,000 as of 12/31/20XX.
>
> b. Actual Net Worth as of 12/31/20XX: $650,000 (In Compliance).

3. *Calculating to confirm compliance.* Remember that good bankers are skeptics, so you should always trust, but verify. Review each of the covenants and do the calculations yourself to be sure that what the borrower reflected in its compliance certificate was accurate.

One reason this process is so critical is you may be the first one to detect when a loan is deteriorating. As you track a borrower's compliance, you may notice a negative monthly trend suggesting that the company may be headed for trouble even if it is currently abiding by its agreement. Or you may see a more obvious problem  when a customer breaches its covenant for the first time. For example, if a borrower's fixed charge coverage ratio is under 1:1 when the loan covenant requires 1.25:1, it's likely that a problem is brewing. Learning to notice these warning signs – "red flags" – and calling them to the attention of others in the bank is a key duty of the Credit Analyst.

Portfolio Metrics

So far in this chapter, I have been discussing how and why banks monitor specific loans after those loans are closed and they move into the repayment phase. Now let's turn our attention from the trees to the forest, stepping back from examining each individual loan and instead thinking about the bank's entire collection (portfolio) of commercial loans.

Since banks are in the business of *managing* risk rather than *avoiding* risk, they know that some of the loans they make will not be repaid as agreed. In fact, the bank that has absolutely no problem loans is not taking *enough* risk. But banks certainly want to minimize the number of their high risk and problem loans. To do this, they must have a way to measure the risk of each loan as well as the risk of the entire loan portfolio.

Banks aren't the only ones who care about measuring and monitoring the overall quality of loan portfolios. Banking regulatory agencies like the Office of the Comptroller of the Currency (OCC), concerned with the safety and soundness of the national banking system, also keep a close eye on how much risk banks are taking in their commercial lending activities. And since many bank stocks are publicly traded, investors want to know they are investing in a bank that can measure and accurately report its credit quality.

Now that you know *why* it is important to be able to measure the overall quality of a bank's loan portfolio, the more important question is, "*How* is this done?" One methodology banking regulators use (and therefore banks also use) is to categorize loans into one of the following classifications (from best to worst):

- Pass
- Watch (not an official classification, but a category used by banks to identify loans on the lowest end of the Pass spectrum)
- Special Mention (also called Other Loans Especially Mentioned or OLEM)
- Substandard
- Doubtful
- Loss

A few more important terms for you to know: loans in any of the four bottom categories (Special Mention or worse) are called "Criticized Assets," and those that are Substandard or worse are referred to as "Classified." I have summarized these regulatory grades and definitions in a diagram at the end of this chapter.

Expected Loss

What is really being measured and categorized here is the "expected loss" on a given loan. The greater the expected loss, the further down the classification list. To understand the concept of expected loss, imagine my three sons, ages nine, seven, and five, climbing three different trees in our back yard. My oldest son is stronger and more experienced than his younger brothers, so the

chances of his falling out of a tree (probability of default) are smaller. But the oldest also likes to climb to the top of the 20-foot tall tree whereas the five-year old prefers to stay on the lower branches. So while his inexperience and weaker hands increase his probability of falling, the magnitude of his injury (loss given default) will be smaller if he does lose his grip.

Probability of default is the risk that a borrower will be unable or unwilling to repay its debt as agreed. This refers to the primary source of repayment of the loan. *Loss given default* (loss in the event of default) is the financial loss a bank suffers when a borrower does not repay. This is based on the outstanding balance of the loan and the collateral as a backup source of repayment. For example, even if a borrower has terribly weak cash flow, the bank's expected loss will be minimal if the loan has only two monthly payments remaining or if the bank is holding cash collateral to support the loan.

Mathematically, this would be expressed as follows:

Probability of Default (PD) X Loss Given Default (LGD)
= Expected Loss (EL)

Since this chapter is about monitoring existing loans, think about how the classification system I just explained helps banks to rate the quality of their commercial loan portfolios. Clearly, banks want most of their loans to be rated *Pass* because this indicates that the bank will be repaid as agreed, earning all of the anticipated interest and fees on those loans. Conversely, banks want to minimize the percentage of Criticized and Classified loans since these are much more likely to result in losses to the bank.

In addition to using the regulatory classifications I've explained, most banks have also developed their own numeric rating models to provide more granularity in their loan grading. For example, since over 90% of the portfolio is typically graded *Pass*, it helps to distinguish between excellent credits with minimal expected loss and satisfactory credits on the lower end of the *Pass* spectrum. These numerical rating systems allow banks to internally upgrade or downgrade credits within their *Pass* category. They therefore also allow for more accurate loan loss provisions since a strong *Pass* credit would require a smaller provision than a loan heading toward *Watch* status.

Going, Going, Gone

One other important reason why banks must accurately and transparently classify each loan in their portfolios is credit loss provisions. As a bank recognizes that an existing loan is deteriorating, it acknowledges that its expected loss on that loan is increasing. To be proactive, the bank should immediately reclassify the loan to accurately reflect its larger expected loss. This process is called "downgrading" the loan. For example, suppose you help underwrite and structure a loan to a new customer. When you receive updated financial statements a year later during the annual review, you notice large operating losses. Or perhaps your covenant compliance review reveals that the borrower has been out of compliance for two consecutive quarters. This would likely result in downgrading the loan from *Pass* to *Special Mention.*

Not only do downgrades give the credit officers a headache, but they also require the bank to set aside more money as a "provision for credit losses." That is, banks do not wait until a borrower actually defaults on a loan to take a loss on that loan. Rather, as it looks more likely that the loan will not be repaid, the bank takes its medicine right away by setting aside more capital to compensate for the expected loss. This provision is an expense on a bank's income statement, so the larger it gets, the greater the negative impact on the bank's earnings (see Figure 1.2 on page 23). Because this process is continually being applied to individual loans, at any point in time the bank can analyze its entire portfolio to see what percentage of its loans fall into each classification.

Elephants, Jugglers, and Bank Loans

You may have learned in Accounting that assets are "what a company owns." For our purposes, I'd like to suggest that assets are those things that allow a company to generate cash flow. If you owned a circus, your primary assets would be trained elephants, jugglers, and trapeze artists. If your elephant broke its leg or your trapeze artist came down with a case of vertigo, no one  would buy circus tickets, and your cash flow would suffer. That is, you would only consider your assets to be "performing" when they were doing what you hired and trained them to do – make you money.

In Chapter 1, I explained that a bank's primary source of revenue is net interest income. Banks earn money when their assets – loans – are performing, or earning interest. Even if principal is repaid as agreed, the bank will lose money if its borrowers are not also making interest payments on their loans. In cases where the borrower has a defined weakness, such as consecutive years of operating losses, it would likely be classified as *Substandard*. And when things get bad enough on a *Substandard* loan that the bank has serious doubts whether it will even recover its principal, then the accounting for the loan changes.

In these situations, when the borrower sends its monthly payment (consisting of principal and interest), the bank applies the entire amount to reducing the principal balance. That is, the bank (internally) tries to accelerate the repayment by applying even the interest being paid to the principal balance. In the eyes of the bank, the loan is no longer earning interest – it has stopped "performing." Don't worry about understanding all of the complex accounting related to these loans. The important take-away is that when the expected loss on a loan is high enough and things are really going downhill, the bank internally labels the loan as a "non-performing asset" (NPA). Clearly, banks want as few NPAs in their portfolios as possible, but they need to be accurate and transparent in identifying and reporting these nasty critters. Regulators, investors, and senior management of the bank want to know what percentage of the portfolio is non-performing and which way this important metric is trending.

Key Takeaways

Credit Monitoring Tools:

- **Annual Reviews**
- **Appraisals**
- **Field Exams**
- **Covenant Compliance Certificates**

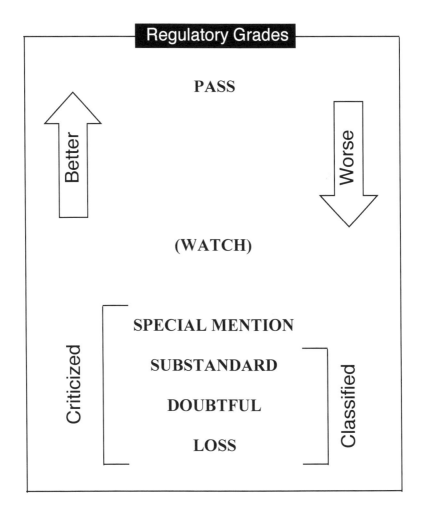

ANDY KEUSAL

Chapter 7

A COMPLEX LENDING MACHINE

I promised you at the beginning of this book that I would give you an insider's view of commercial banking and how you can best prepare yourself to successfully break into it. By now, you should have at least a high-level understanding of how the business works. I've covered how banks make money; why businesses borrow; how loans are underwritten, structured, and approved; and what happens after loans are booked.

But if you want to be fully prepared to jump into this career and hit the ground running, you also need to know a little about the other parts of the bank and how they fit into the big picture. I told you at the outset that banking is first and foremost a relationship business, and your most important relationships will be those with your co-workers. To that end, in this chapter I will introduce you to some other departments in the bank. I will explain what each of these groups does and how you will interact with them. This is one area where most new commercial bankers are completely in the dark, so having this knowledge from the beginning will give you a huge competitive advantage. It will also help you to have more impactful interactions with management, thus accelerating your career advancement.

Like any large business, the bank where you work will have departments that employ people who aren't necessarily bankers: Human Resources (HR), Information Technology (IT), Accounting, Operations, Marketing, Communications (Public Relations), and Facilities. The people who work in these parts of the bank are critical to the bank's success, but they don't usually have an in-depth knowledge of commercial banking, nor do they have to.

In this chapter I want to focus my attention on the parts of the bank that are most closely related to your role in commercial banking. I have already mentioned some of these in previous chapters, but now I will explain a bit more about what each group does and what you need to know about them. After a brief discussion about retail banking, I will cover:

- Credit Administration
- Commercial Lending
- Commercial Real Estate
- Leasing
- Collateral Services
- Private Banking

- Special Loans
- Loan Review
- Treasury Management
- Legal
- Government Regulators

Rah, Rah Retail!

In Chapter 1, I made a distinction between retail and commercial banking. This book is obviously about the commercial side, but since most people are familiar only with retail, I want to spend a moment there. When I say "retail banking," think of branches and ATMs. If you were to ask most people to name the three largest banks in your hometown, they would probably quickly list those banks that have the most branches on the busiest city streets. Many people are not even aware that these banks have corporate offices in town, and if they do it's only because the banks have their names in lights atop the downtown skyscrapers. And virtually no one has a clue what happens inside the walls of those corporate banking office buildings.

Retail banking is critical to the success of any bank franchise because those who work in branches are the face of the bank to the public. Tellers are expected to answer any question a customer has, including handling problem situations and people who are irate because they think their money has been mishandled. Branch managers and personal bankers not only have to oversee thousands of customer transactions every week. They are also responsible for opening new accounts and selling home mortgages, home equity lines of credit, and numerous other consumer banking products and services. All of this is valuable work experience because it helps you see banking through a typical customer's eyes, develops your sales and interpersonal skills, and introduces you to many of the bank's operating systems.

Many of my readers are people who are currently working in the retail side of a bank. I have heard from many people who have been through this retail learning curve and now want to transition into commercial but don't know how to get there. If you are in that situation, trust me when I tell you that your experience in the branch will be a great asset to you when you make the move to commercial. I have interviewed, hired, and trained hundreds of new Credit Analysts, and some of the most successful ones were people who came directly from the retail part of the bank. Along with the information in this book, your skills and banking experience give you a significant competitive advantage over many of your peers entering the commercial banking field.

Credit Administration

While there are many different functions and job titles within commercial banking, I have focused most of my attention in this book on the role of the Credit Analyst. The reason why I have explained things through the lens of the Credit Analyst is that this is the most common starting point for most people who work on the commercial side of the bank. "Credit is King," and wherever you want to take your commercial banking career, you won't get far without a solid background in credit.

The size and scope of the Credit department varies based on the organization for which you work. In larger banks, a number of Credit Analysts all typically report to a Credit Manager or to a Senior Credit Officer. You may also work with Portfolio Managers (PMs) who assist the commercial lenders in handling their existing relationships, thus freeing up the lenders' time to focus on prospecting and winning new business. In smaller institutions, you may wear many hats and might act as both Analyst and Portfolio Manager. Some banks have "Loan Underwriters" whose job functions are very similar to those of an Analyst. In some cases, these two titles are synonymous, and in others the differentiation is based on the market segment served – Large Corporate, Middle Market, or Business Banking relationships (defined in the next section).

Commercial Lending

Those bankers whose job is focused on prospecting and building new customer relationships are referred to as Lenders, Relationship Managers (RMs), Bankers, or even "the line." The latter term comes from differentiating between those who have regular customer contact on the "front line" versus those who spend most of their time "behind the line" in the office like Analysts and Portfolio Managers. Many banks now prefer the title *Relationship Manager* to *Lender* because these bankers no longer focus only on lending. Rather, they are the primary point of contact with customers for both loans and other bank products. Clearly, these Relationship Managers must enjoy the sales process, have strong interpersonal and credit skills, and show a lot of patience.

Why patience? As I told you in Chapter 5, the process of courting a new business customer often takes years. Successful Relationship Managers devote much time and energy to attending evening social events, building relationships with centers of influence like CPAs and attorneys, and, yes, golfing. Unlike the stereotypical car salesperson, a commercial lender may only "close" a handful of deals every year, but each one is well earned and adds meaningful profitability to the bank.

You should also know that some lenders are "generalists" who call on customers in any and all industries. This is usually called "Commercial & Industrial" lending (C&I). Others specialize in one area such as commercial real estate, technology, or health care.

Commercial lending teams are also often segmented by the *size* of the companies they service. Larger banks distinguish among these segments as follows:

- Large Corporate Lending – for businesses with revenues in billions, including publicly traded companies

- Middle Market (or Corporate) Lending – companies with revenues from tens of millions to hundreds of millions
- Business Banking – companies with revenues in millions

Start-ups and smaller businesses (not large enough to qualify for Business Banking) are typically managed by retail bankers or by lenders who specialize in SBA lending. These SBA loans are usually too risky to be typical bank deals, so banks structure them with the support of a government guarantee from the U.S. Small Business Administration, thus allowing the business to borrow money without the bank having to take excessive risk.

Commercial Real Estate

Loans for the purpose of financing commercial real estate require specialization due to their uniqueness and complexity. Because almost all banks make these CRE loans, they require expertise in real estate appraisal, construction financing, and environmental issues. This segment includes buildings that are owner-occupied as well as investment properties such as office, retail, and residential apartments.

Leasing

Sometimes called "Equipment Finance," this group works with

customers to finance capital expenditures through capital leasing arrangements. That is, instead of making a term loan to a borrower to purchase equipment, the bank actually buys the equipment and then "rents" it to the customer. Customers like this option because they often get lower interest rates and can sometimes finance 90-100% of the cost of the equipment, versus a smaller percentage when financing through term debt. As you might guess, bankers who work in Equipment Finance have expertise in all types of big, expensive machinery, vehicles, and aircraft.

Collateral Services

I mentioned this group when I discussed monitoring existing loans, but they are so important that I want to explain their role in more detail here. In the first bank where I worked, this team sat just down the hall from my workstation, but since they were rarely in the office, I never got to know any of them. Finally I asked my manager, "Who are those guys?" I was told that they were the "Secured Credit" group, also known as *Field Exam* or *Collateral Monitoring Services*. The reason they were rarely around is that their job was to be in our customers' places of business verifying the value of our collateral.

Here is how it works: imagine that the bank extends a $3,000,000 working capital line of credit to a customer. As you already know, the purpose of the line of credit would be for the company to purchase inventory and pay its expenses while waiting to collect its accounts receivable from its customers – "working capital financing." While banks trust their customers, they should still verify what their customers tell them. So in this example, the bank would want to be sure that its customer has sufficient collateral – inventory and accounts receivable – to support the outstanding balance on the line. The customer may report having $3,000,000 of inventory and $4,000,000 of accounts receivable. But the bank's credit officers will sleep better at night once the field examiners have spent time on site counting the boxes in the warehouse and confirming the collectability of the company's IOUs.

Like Credit Analysts, Field Examiners must have good credit skills, a solid accounting background, and a keen eye for detecting when something doesn't look right. In the course of routine field exams (collateral audits), these bankers can uncover mismanagement, poor inventory controls, and in rare cases, fraud. If detected early enough, these problems can be addressed, potentially avoiding large future credit losses.

Private Banking

If you start your commercial banking career working in Business Banking or Middle Market Lending, most of the companies you bank will be privately owned by individuals or families. Since some of these businesses generate significant profits, the families that own them can become quite wealthy. Bankers affectionately refer to these business owners as "certified rich people." It might surprise you to know that many wealthy people like to borrow money. They develop expensive hobbies, invest in other businesses, and purchase vacation homes, so they frequently borrow for these purposes rather than using their own cash.

Extending credit to an individual is very different than underwriting a commercial loan, but your bank will want to do both, especially when the individual has a proven track record of success in business. Wealthy people, including business owners, corporate executives, and professionals, may or may not have borrowing needs. But they still need financial and investment advice. Whether it's called the Wealth Group, Private Client Services, or Private Banking, most large banks have a group of lenders and investment advisors who specialize in servicing this unique segment of customers.

What's So *Special* About *These* Loans?

Have you ever invested time and energy planning a special event that still turned out to be a disaster? Even when you have all of the bases covered and you have anticipated all possible obstacles, things can go terribly wrong. And so it is in commercial banking. Every experienced banker can tell you his favorite "spilled milk" story about a promising deal that went sour. When loans are made, borrowers have every intention of repaying them, and bankers certainly expect to be repaid. But a lot can happen during the repayment period: economic cycles, competition, management changes, and, yes, fraud.

Whatever the cause, loans that are thoroughly underwritten and properly structured can still hit icebergs and begin to take on water. Technically speaking, loans that are graded *Pass* sometimes deteriorate into *Special Mention* and *Substandard* credits. In many of these instances, the borrower is still  making all loan payments on time. But if the bank's expected loss increases to where the loan becomes Criticized or Classified, it's time to call for help. Most banks now manage these bad loans through a group called "Special Loans," "Workout," or "Problem Assets." The people who work on these teams are typically smart, experienced bankers with good street sense. Their goal is to either rehabilitate the customer so the loans can start "performing" again or exit the relationship, helping the customer to find another bank.

Loan Review

Every good bank needs strong "internal controls" – people working for the bank who check to be sure that all processes are being followed correctly. The Loan Review or Credit Review department serves this independent audit function by doing periodic exams and issuing reports to share its findings. What exactly does Loan Review examine? All of the things we've looked at in Chapters 3 through 6:

- Are loan requests being underwritten and structured according to the bank's written credit policies?
- Is the bank rating its commercial loans accurately in accordance with regulatory classifications?
- Is the bank tracking and reporting covenant compliance in a timely manner?
- Are loan requests being approved by those with appropriate credit authority?

Since Loan Review examines both Credit Administration and the various lending segments, it typically does not report to either of these groups but is separate and distinct from each. As an objective third party within the bank, it shares the results of its exams with bank regulators, the accounting firm that audits the bank, and the bank's Board of Directors.

Treasury Management

Since most new commercial bankers start their careers in a credit role, I have spent most of this book explaining to you the key components of the credit approval process. But as I told you in Chapter 1, net interest income isn't the only source of revenue for banks. They also sell products to earn fees, and much of that non-interest income comes from Treasury Management or Cash Management products. Most businesses need more than a simple checking account to manage their cash flow. Although banks offer numerous Treasury Management products and services to their commercial customers, I'll keep it simple by explaining three of the most common products.

- *Automated Clearing House (ACH)* – If you have ever had your monthly rent or gym membership electronically withdrawn from your checking account or received a paycheck by direct deposit, then you are a user of ACH products. The company that accepted your monthly payment or sent your paycheck directly to your account needed a bank to provide that service, and it paid the bank a fee to do so.

- *Lockbox* – Have you ever mailed a check to a company to pay for a product or a monthly service bill? Although bills are increasingly paid using online banking, imagine how many checks your electric company still receives each month from its customers. Have you ever noticed that the mailing address of the electric company is usually a P.O. Box? What most consumers don't realize is that their checks are not being sent to the utility company but rather directly to that company's bank. The bank then collects thousands of those checks each day and immediately deposits them into the utility company's checking account, saving it time and, more importantly, getting those funds into the bank more quickly. Most businesses that receive a large number of paper checks are happy to pay their bank a fee for this "lockbox" service.

- *Remote Deposit Capture* – What about the business that receives only a few dozen checks each day but is located miles from its bank's nearest branch? Instead of making its customers waste time driving to a branch to deposit checks, banks offer their commercial customers portable check scanners. These convenient devices allow the company to quickly capture images of each check and deposit them into the company's account remotely without ever leaving the office. Many banks are now beginning to offer this convenience to their retail customers as well.

Legal

I suspect you have heard (or told) jokes like, "What is black and brown and looks good on a lawyer? A Doberman!" While lawyer

jokes still abound, unfortunately bankers are frequently now the punch lines, especially since some people blame us for the recent financial collapse. So what could be funnier than lawyers who work at a bank?!

Banks, like any other businesses, do get sued. When companies borrow money and eventually struggle to repay, banks reluctantly resort to liquidating collateral or enforcing personal guarantees. Do the banks have a legal right to these courses of action? Of course they do. Do their customers still sue them for doing so? Occasionally they do, and that's why banks need an internal legal staff – attorneys who are knowledgeable in both law and commercial banking. While some of the bank's lawyers are busy in court, others are needed for more internal purposes such as reviewing the language used in covenants and other loan agreements. All kidding aside, good banks need good lawyers, and you will benefit from getting to know those who work at your institution.

Government Regulators

This is the group that will catch you most by surprise when you begin working for a bank. You may have heard that banking is a "highly regulated industry," but what exactly does this mean? Many industries have governing bodies that establish and enforce how their business is to be conducted. Medical doctors must answer to the American Medical Association (AMA); accountants abide by Financial Accounting Standards Board (FASB) rulings; even lawyers can be disbarred by the American Bar Association if they don't play by their own rules.

But because government organizations oversee banking regulations and because banks deal with individuals' and companies' *money*, the oversight is especially stringent. Since the crash of 2008, regulatory agencies have cited banks' missteps to justify their ever-increasing presence and influence.

The three primary regulatory agencies involved with commercial banking are:

- *Office of the Comptroller of the Currency* (OCC) – A U.S. federal agency that charters, regulates, and supervises national banks. The OCC monitors the asset quality, capital levels, and liquidity of banks to ensure they are operating safely.

- *Federal Reserve System* (Fed) – The central bank of the United States. Originally created to stabilize the banking system, the Fed also sets monetary policy through its Federal Open Market Committee (FOMC) and regulates banking through its twelve regional Federal Reserve Banks.

- *Federal Deposit Insurance Corporation* (FDIC) – Founded in 1933 after the stock market crash of 1929 to insure deposits in U.S. banks against bank failure. The FDIC also examines some banks for financial safety and soundness.

For better or worse, these agencies are here to stay, and they will continue to take active roles in monitoring and supervising banks in our country. Decades ago, a bank might expect to have a visit from a bank examiner annually, expecting a high-level review of the bank's commercial loan portfolio. Now the examinations are much more frequent and significantly more thorough. It is not uncommon for regulators to establish permanent offices for themselves within the corridors of a bank, allowing ample time and opportunity to zoom in with unprecedented scrutiny on loan portfolios, specific segments, and even specific loan facilities.

Again, many would argue that this level of government monitoring is appropriate given the impact of the financial crisis of 2008. Plenty of bankers, on the other hand, see it as an unnecessary intrusion that costs both banks and taxpayers money. My purpose here is simply to open your eyes to the reality of the regulatory environment into which you are stepping and to remind you that your manager won't be the only one looking over your shoulder.

Summary

As you can see, commercial banking is indeed a pretty complex network of diverse people and functions. You certainly don't need to remember and understand all I have explained to you in this long chapter. In fact, a lot of this won't make sense until you are actually on the job and beginning to interact with these groups. Use this chapter as a reference for when you encounter people who work in these various capacities, and you will find that you are much better prepared than your counterparts to put all of the pieces of the commercial banking puzzle together. Knowing how each piece fits into the bigger picture will help you to understand your own role better and will allow you to work more effectively with each of the groups I've described here. You will know whom to go to with specific questions or problems, and solidifying these internal connections will make you a better candidate when promotional opportunities arise. The next chapter will help you understand your potential career paths in greater detail.

Who They Are and What They Do

Credit	*Approving the risks*
Lending	*Winning new customers*
Commercial Real Estate	*Financing bricks and sticks*
Leasing	*Financing heavy equipment*
Collateral Services	*Trusting but verifying*
Private Banking	*Wooing the wealthy*
Special Loans	*Rehabilitating the wounded (assets)*
Loan Review	*Checking and reporting*
Treasury Management	*Generating fee income*
Legal	*Defending and protecting*
Regulators	*Looking over your shoulder*

Chapter 8

A DAY IN THE LIFE

Way to go! Having gotten to this last chapter, you have proven that you are serious about breaking into commercial banking. Others may, like you, have a Finance degree with a high grade point average or even experience working in a bank branch. But you now also have an insider's perspective on what really happens on the commercial side of a bank, and you know far more about how banking really works than other candidates competing for the job. Although each of the subjects we've covered could be explored in a lot more depth, at least you can now talk intelligently about the key people, processes, and products that make a commercial banking engine run.

But I promised you more than just *information* about banking – I want you to feel completely prepared to jump in and be successful. Knowledge is indeed power *if you know how to apply that knowledge.* To that end, I want to wrap up with three must-know answers to key questions that will help you get your foot in the door and keep you on the right track:

- How can I interview well to increase my chances of getting hired?
- What should I expect a typical day to look like when I get started?
- How do I navigate my career path?

None of what I've explained to you in the first seven chapters will be of any value to you if you can't get hired into the commercial banking position you want. Interviewing is so important and yet so simple that I've broken it out as a separate Bonus Chapter immediately after this one.

Test-Drive Your New Job

You are about to enter a new career field, and before you invest time, money, and energy into it, you want to be sure that you are a good fit. I have interviewed hundreds of candidates for commercial banking positions, and one of the most commonly asked questions is, "What would I expect to do in a typical day at work?" The answer to this question is important – you want to be sure you know what you are signing up for. I have spoken to a number of hiring managers at banks recently who shared with me that their greatest frustration is watching new employees flounder in their first year because they really aren't in the right job. Candidates may have had the right major in college and sincerely believed that banking was the career for them. But once they actually started doing the job, they realized it wasn't at all what they thought it would be.

I don't believe that will happen to you because you have tasted all this book has to offer, and you're still hungry for more! So while a "typical" day will look somewhat different depending on which bank you work for, let's walk through a day in your life as a relatively new Credit Analyst, and let's be sure your new banking shoes fit comfortably before you buy them.

Your day starts as you arrive at your desk early to review all your tasks for the day. You will have a number of credit requests on your desk at any given time, so time management skills are vital. The piles in your workstation include some annual reviews, covenant compliance checks, and a new loan request for a prospective customer that a Relationship Manager has been courting for two years. Prioritizing these items will help your day to run more smoothly.

At 8:30 a.m., you report to the large conference room where Credit Committee is held every Tuesday and Thursday morning. The Committee will be discussing seven different deals this morning, and one of them is an annual review that you wrote last week. You want to hear the discussion, and you may even get an opportunity to show what you know if a question is asked of you.

In this case, the Relationship Manager who handles this customer answers the few questions members of the committee ask her, and you remain a spectator. As so often happens, your behind-the-scenes work on the credit report goes relatively unnoticed, but the lack of any omissions or errors in your written document speaks to your thoroughness and strong attention to detail. In these situations, it's good *not* to be noticed.

As soon as you return to your desk from Credit Committee, your favorite Portfolio Manager meets you with a "rush" request. He tells you that he accompanied a Relationship Manager on a prospect call yesterday afternoon, and the company agreed to provide financial statements to your bank in hopes of borrowing money for a new project. Your task is to input the numbers from the company's statements into your bank's statement spreading software (spread the numbers) as quickly as possible because the RM and PM want to informally discuss the numbers with their credit officer in a 10:00 a.m. meeting. You were planning to work on your other new loan request this morning, but now you must reprioritize your day to accommodate this unexpected request.

With this done, you turn your attention to the new loan request. A company that does plastic injection molding wants to borrow money for an expensive piece of new equipment, and you are tasked with identifying the key credit risks in the deal. In scanning the information provided, you learn that the customer provides parts to the automotive industry. You remember that this morning's *Wall Street Journal* had an article about the current state of the auto industry, so you quickly review that article to get up to speed. Plastic injection molding, however, is completely new to you, so before you can dive into your deal, you need to do some industry research. You don't need to be an expert, but you do need to understand this process so you will better grasp why the company would want to purchase the equipment. This kind of industry information is readily available online, and your bank may also subscribe to online industry research tools, which will help you identify key issues pertinent to your borrower.

Your research is going well, and now you think you'll be able to tackle everything on your "to do" list by the end of the day. But you are interrupted by another RM who has stopped by your desk asking you to join her and her PM for a lunch meeting with one of her customers. An existing customer of the bank, this real estate developer has asked the bank to finance a large apartment complex he wants to build. Since you will be assigned to write the credit report on this request, the RM thought it would be helpful for you to meet the borrower and visit the site of the proposed project. You know this meeting will throw your day completely off schedule, but it will be worth it to get out of the office and meet your borrower in person. And since real estate projects are all about location, a site visit will definitely allow you to write a more complete, accurate report.

On the ride back to the office, you participate in an informal "underwriting preview" conversation with the RM and PM. They quickly summarize the developer's strong reputation in the industry and his solid borrowing history with your bank. They review the projected occupancy rates that the developer provided. You are able to share some insight into market demographics since the proposed apartments would be near another complex where many of your friends currently live. The discussion then turns to whether the developer's global cash flow from his other projects will be sufficient to make this new loan without requiring his guarantee. The RM and PM agree that 220 bps would be an appropriate spread, and you wonder, "How they could know that already?" Seeing the quizzical look on your face, the RM simply says, "We've been doing this a while – you just know." Peppering them with more questions, you feverishly take notes, knowing you will never remember all of these details when you sit down to write your underwriting summary tomorrow.

What is left of your day is spent writing. You now have two new loan requests to work on, and both of them require a first draft

of a credit report within 48 hours. After crunching a few numbers, you begin to formulate some initial thoughts about the risks in each deal, and now it's time to put your thoughts on paper. You have collected so much data, and you have so much to say. Which facts are the most pertinent, and how can you present them in the clearest way? You know that in business writing, brevity is best, so you strive to say as much as possible in a few brief paragraphs, adding some bullet points and a financial chart or two to support your conclusions.

Only your hunger draws your attention to the clock, and you realize it's already 6:15 p.m. by the time you finish your writing. You have juggled your priorities well, and even after a few months on the job, it still surprises you how much you learn on each new deal. The day seems to fly by, but you are never bored, and you are building valuable relationships, earning a good reputation within the bank by your responsiveness, humility, and work ethic. Congratulations – you have cracked the code and broken into banking!

Where Do I Go from Here?

I have focused my discussion in this chapter on the role of a Credit Analyst because that is the role in which commercial bankers usually enter the field. This job is demanding, challenging, and time-consuming. It is a terrific learning experience, and most successful bankers will tell you that they earned their stripes by working as a Credit Analyst in their early years. But most people don't stay in this role for more than two years. You pay your dues while you are on the lowest rung of the corporate ladder, knowing that your day for advancement and greater pay will come. As you gain experience and build relationships with others in your bank, other opportunities will eventually open up for you, especially if you learn quickly and master the basics.

There really is no prescribed career path after your first banking job, especially because each bank is structured differently. Also, each person reading this book will have varying interests and abilities. As you perform well in your Credit Analyst role, your bank may promote you to a Senior Credit Analyst position where you work on more complex loan requests and even begin to help some of the newer analysts.

Few people remain in the Credit Analyst role more than two years. Your next role is most commonly a junior Portfolio Manager (PM) or Relationship Manager (RM) role, depending on

how your bank is structured and on your appetite for prospecting. RMs spend much of their time out of the office calling on prospective customers, expanding their social and professional networks. Some institutions have their RMs prospect for new business *and* manage the portfolio of their existing customers as well. Many banks, however, also have PMs – people with good credit backgrounds who enjoy some customer contact but don't enjoy prospecting and having to win new business for the bank. Unlike RMs, PMs spend most of their working hours in the office where they monitor and manage existing relationships. Frequently the RM, PM, and Credit Analyst work as a "deal team," each filling a specific role in the underwriting, structuring, closing, and monitoring of each lending relationship. It is a natural career progression, then, for a successful Credit Analyst to step up into a junior PM or RM position.

Having read these job descriptions, you may have a sense of what your next step will be, but I recommend you stay flexible and wait to see what kinds of opportunities present themselves. I have hired many people who start as Credit Analysts, knowing that they want to be Relationship Managers. But after a year or two on the job and really seeing what each role entails, they frequently change their minds and gravitate to something else within the bank. Many people demonstrate strong analytical skills, build solid internal relationships, and are well thought of across the bank; but neither the RM nor PM role appeals to them as a next step.

If you end up in this situation, you will have an even greater appreciation for the relationships you have built with others around the bank in your first year or two. Remember this: every interaction you have with other bankers, especially members of senior management, is an interview for your next position. When you are in the car debriefing your customer call with an RM and PM, you are interviewing. When you get into the elevator with the Director of Commercial Real Estate, you are interviewing. And yes, when you are at the Christmas party mingling with an Executive Vice President, you are interviewing. If you learn to always think this way, you will be well positioned for the next open spot, wherever in the bank it may be.

What do these opportunities look like? Consider the following typical scenarios:

- In the midst of a chaotic day, you slow down just enough to take note of something that didn't look right on a customer's financial statements. You raise a red flag and ask for help from a peer in the Special Loans group, resulting in the early detection of a problem loan. This might be the start of your career as a workout officer.

- Your insightful questions on a customer call lead to an RM requesting you to be his analyst on all of his complex deals from then on. Once you become the analyst of choice, your workload may be heavier than that of your fellow analysts since you will be assigned more deals, but it's worth it. When that RM has an opening on his team, you won't even need a formal interview. He will call you and ask if you are interested in joining his team, and your career as a commercial lender will have taken a huge step forward.

And don't forget about Credit Administration. If working as a Credit Analyst captures your imagination but you want to take on more responsibility and ultimately have the power of the pen, other opportunities exist to advance within the Credit department. Every Chief Credit Officer once spent time as a new Credit Analyst; every Senior Underwriter once spent time spreading financial statements and working long hours writing credit reports.

The same can be said for any of the groups I described in the Chapter 7. You may have no idea when a job opportunity will arise in Private Banking, Collateral Services, Commercial Real Estate, or Loan Review. But I can promise you that when it does, having a strong credit background on your resume will vault your name to the top of the candidate list. If you have proven to be a team player, demonstrated good writing skills, and impressed people with your desire and ability to learn, you will have laid a rock-solid foundation for a long, prosperous banking career.

Key Takeaways

Traits of a Successful Credit Analyst:

- **Time Management Skills**
- **Sincere Interest in Business**
- **Willingness and Ability to Learn**
- **Humility**
- **Curiosity**
- **Responsiveness**
- **Analytical Ability**
- **Business Writing Skills**
- **Flexibility**
- **Interpersonal Communication Skills**
- **Patience**
- **Willingness to Work Hard**

ANDY KEUSAL

Bonus Chapter

INTERVIEW TIPS
FROM AN INDUSTRY INSIDER

Assuming that you didn't skip immediately to this section of the book first, you now have insight into all facets of commercial banking, particularly the entry-level role of a Credit Analyst. I trust that what you have read confirms that this is the right industry for you and you now feel confident in understanding what your job duties will actually be.

But wanting a job isn't the same as having one (unless your father happens to be on the Board of Directors of your favorite bank). Whether you are graduating from school, currently working in the retail side of a bank, or coming to banking from another industry, you will need to successfully interview to win the commercial banking job you want.

But wouldn't you like to know exactly what to say to set yourself apart from other candidates? As much as you want to get that offer letter, the bank wants to fill its open position with the most qualified person. During the interview, both sides are selling.

So how can you quickly and convincingly close the deal?

Don't Try This....

I will never forget sitting across the desk from a graduating college senior in the interview room at one of the nation's best business schools. The candidate was majoring in Finance and Accounting and had a respectable GPA, and the interview was progressing well. After explaining the salient points of the job to him, I asked, "What do you hope to gain from working for our bank?" With an air of relaxed confidence, he leaned back in his chair, clicked his tongue, and pointed at me (as if to fire the winning shot with his air pistol), and said, "Benefits!"

On another occasion I had risen early in the morning to make the 2-hour drive from my home to the career center at a prestigious local university. I was schedule to interview a dozen students between 8:00 a.m. and 4:30 p.m., so I left early enough to arrive at my destination by 7:45. Once settled in my interview room, I walked to the waiting area and called the name of my first candidate. A bleary-eyed young man rose from his chair and followed me down the hall. As we walked to our room, I noticed that his hair was uncombed, and it appeared that he had thrown himself into his business suit and tie with some haste. "Are you OK?" I asked, sensing that his day was off to a rough start. "I'm pretty wiped out," he confided. "Yesterday was my 21st birthday, and my buddies took me out last night. Great time, but I was out pretty late," he moaned, rubbing his unshaven face. I mercifully excused him from the interview, wondering why he would have invested four years and thousands of dollars only to squander this precious opportunity for gainful employment.

But the most memorable conversation of all happened to a fellow hiring manager who was wrapping up what she thought was a very promising interview with a young lady. When asked why she had singled out our bank as her top choice, the candidate replied, "I want to work for a large and stable company, and your bank is unsinkable. You are like the Titanic!"

I'm not making this stuff up. And believe me, I could go on. These comical interactions, perhaps the result of a lack of preparation and some nervousness, represent the worst of the worst. Most interviews are slightly better, but very few are good enough to accomplish your primary objective: to have the bank put your name at the top of their candidate list. I have interviewed, hired, and trained hundreds of people just like you, so I know what the banks want. Follow these simple guidelines, and you will make memorable impressions *for the right reasons*, paving the way for you to successfully break into banking.

Prove That You Want the Job

This tip is worth more than all of the others combined: *you need to convince your interviewer that you have a sincere interest in commercial banking.* I don't offer this as a gimmick to help you get hired. I know (because you are reading this book) that your interest is genuine; now you must demonstrate this to your potential employer. All of us who have struggled to train employees who didn't work out know that the single biggest reason for failure is that the employee simply isn't interested in the work.

Commercial banking is about creating relationships with businesses so that you can take appropriate risk by knowing when and how to extend credit to those companies. To do this successfully, you must really want to understand what the business does, how it serves its customers, and how it will be able to repay its loans. Even with your strong academic background, you can't possibly know all you need to know about manufacturing, distribution, real estate, professional practices, yield curves, business writing, financial accounting, and the competitive banking market. But you *can* demonstrate your desire to *learn* these things. Here are some suggestions how you can do this:

1) **Read** – Gain insights into business and into the banking industry by subscribing to publications and staying current on issues. I recommend *The Wall Street Journal* for general business and economic news and *The RMA Journal* and *American Banker* for articles specific to banking. The Risk Management Association (RMA) has been around for 100 years and is the leading industry organization for banking and risk management professionals. *American*

Banker was first published in 1835 and is a leading information source for the banking and financial services industries. Your small financial investment in these magazines, and your demonstration of having read them, will show your desire to learn your trade. And since you have invested money and time in studying this book, bring a copy to your interview and highlight a few key things you have learned.

2) **Study** – You know by now the importance of financial accounting, business writing, and interpersonal skills in furthering your success as a banker. Why not invest in a self-study course in one or all of these areas? Doing so would again demonstrate that you are serious about growing professionally. More importantly, it would give you the skills and knowledge so critical to your upward mobility. For less than what it cost to buy your first interview suit, you could invest in these foundational career building blocks. If you aren't sure where to find resources on these topics, see my "Recommended Resources" page at the end of this book, or go to the Resources page on BreakingIntoBanking.com.

Finally, if you truly want to differentiate yourself and nail the interview, I recommend buying my online course, "Breaking Into

Banking." The modules in this course explore the topics covered in this book in much greater depth and will prepare you to succeed on the job better than any other resource I have seen. You will literally have a six-month head start on your peers, allowing you to hit the ground running and to move through your bank's training program smoothly and rapidly. And if you work for a bank that does not offer a formal credit training program, my course will be an even more invaluable tool for you.

In all my years of interviewing people, I have never met a candidate who had invested his or her own time and money in these kinds of resources. Taking these steps will not guarantee your getting a job from every interview, but it will certainly increase your chances. More importantly, doing the things I have suggested will prepare you to thrive on the job once you are hired.

Bonus Tips

These additional Dos and Don'ts will add a little icing on the cake and improve your odds even more.

<u>Do:</u> Exhibit confidence. A firm handshake and good eye contact are a good start.

> <u>Don't:</u> Be arrogant or overbearing. Eye contact doesn't mean a stare-down, and bone-crushing handshakes don't impress anyone. Your confidence should flow naturally from your preparation and sincerity; gimmicks and pretense

are unnecessary and ineffective.

Do: Express your uniqueness and be remembered for good reasons.

> Don't: Be weird just to be noticed. There is a fine line here; if you aren't sure about disclosing something, ask a parent or trusted advisor if it's appropriate. I still remember the guy who spent extra money printing his resume on cardboard stock with a glossy finish, but spent the first five minutes of the interview telling me about the haircut he got just for this interview. The rest of the interview was merely a formality.

Do: Demonstrate your sincere interest in banking and business.

> Don't: Neglect to mention your other interests. One of the best people I ever hired had a Finance degree and a good GPA, but what won me over was that he had earned a private pilot's license during his college years. This showed dedication and patience, convincing me that he was interesting and well-rounded.

Do: Research the bank and know specifically why you want to work there.

> Don't: Shortcut. Many times I have asked candidates why they are interested in working for us versus other banks. Too many times, the response is something like, "I noticed

that your asset size is $XX billion, and your stock price just jumped to $X.XX." Rather than spending 60 seconds online updating these facts, learn something specific and pertinent. Examples might be, "I have heard positive comments about your training program from other people who work here" or, "I may want to eventually specialize in Commercial Real Estate, and I know your bank has a terrific reputation in that segment." Some of this information may be on the bank's website, or you may have to ask around and find someone who works there to learn it, but it's worth the extra effort.

Do: Follow up in writing, and then by phone.

Don't: Be mechanical or generic. Even though you are probably interviewing with more than one bank, give the impression that this one is your first choice and explain how the interview confirmed this. The typical "Thank you and I look forward to hearing back from you" is best replaced by "Your training program and the potential career paths you laid out for me match exactly what I am looking for to begin my commercial banking career. Your bank is at the top of my list, and I plan to call you next week to discuss next steps."

Recommended Resources for Further Learning

Business Writing, Grammar, Presentations, and Interpersonal Communication Skills:

    Comerford Consulting   Indianapolis, IN
    On the web: comerfordconsulting.com
    Contact info: linda@comerfordconsulting.com
               (317) 786-6404

Financial Accounting for Bankers:

    Edge Development Group   Pittsburgh, PA
    On the web: EdgeDevelopment.com
    Contact info: questions@EdgeDevelopment.com
               (412) 343-0105

Industry Reading:

    The *Wall Street Journal* newspaper
    On the web: online.wsj.com

    RMA Journal magazine
    On the web: rmahq.org/tools-publications/the-rma-journal

    American Banker magazine
    On the web: AmericanBanker.com/magazine

Visit BREAKINGINTOBANKING.COM

to access these **free resources:**

➢ RECEIVE a copy of Andy's current *Special Report*

➢ WATCH an introductory video and sample lesson from the online *Breaking into Banking* course

➢ REGISTER for a webinar hosted by Andy Keusal:

"How to Get Ahead in Your Banking Job

Before You Even Start"

For information about coaching programs

or to contact the author:

andy@keusallearning.com

(614) 634-1474

ABOUT THE AUTHOR

Andy Keusal is passionate about using his teaching gift to help others reach their God-given potential. He spent 18 years in commercial banking, during which he interviewed, hired, and trained hundreds of new bankers. He also helped build and run one of the nation's premier credit training programs at a large Midwest regional bank. He left his corporate career in 2015 to found Keusal Learning, where he now helps people master the basics of banking. Many of his trainees have moved on to prosperous careers in banking, private equity, and even business ownership.

As a husband and father of nine children, Andy devotes much of his time and energy to helping his wife Kirsten educate their eight children still living at home. Ordained as an Elder in the Covenant Presbyterian Church, Andy is also actively involved in his local church. The Keusal family lives on a five-acre homestead in central Ohio.

Made in the USA
Charleston, SC
09 December 2016